C000010641

ERRIGAL

SACRED MOUNTAIN

About the Author

Cathal Ó Searcaigh was born and grew up on a hill farm in Mín an Leá, Gort an Choirce, an Irish-speaking glen and Gaeltacht community in the northwest of County Donegal. The author of 20 volumes of poetry, three plays and four works of prose in Irish, as well as four books in English, he is a leading figure in the remarkable renaissance of Irish-language writing in our time. He is a member of Aosdána, and continues to live on the home ground of his parents.

ERRIGAL

SACRED MOUNTAIN

CATHAL Ó SEARCAIGH

THE IRISH PAGES PRESS
CLÓ AN MHÍL BHUÍ
2023

Errigal: Sacred Mountain
is first published in hardback on 15 August 2023.

The Irish Pages Press
129 Ormeau Road
Belfast BT7 1SH
Ireland

www.irishpages.org

Editors: Chris Agee and Jacob Agee

Copyright © Cathal Ó Searcaigh & The Irish Pages Press

All rights reserved. No part of this book may be reproduced,
stored in a retrieval system, or transmitted in any form,
or by any means, electronic, mechanical, photocopying or otherwise,
without prior written permission from The Irish Pages Press.

Typeset in 14/18 pt Monotype Perpetua.
Designed and composed by RV, Belfast. Printed by Bell & Bain, Glasgow.

A CIP catalogue record for this book
is available from The British Library.

Dust-jacket photographs: "Tranquil Errigal" by Derek Smyth,
and author's portrait by Reuben Ó Conluain.

ISBN: 978-1-7393537-1-1

This book has been generously funded by Donegal County Council, Ealaín na Gaeltachta,
Pleanáil Teanga, Údarás na Gaeltachta, The Arts Council of Ireland and Creative Ireland.

Also by Cathal Ó Searcaigh

PROSE

Tulach Beaglaoich: Inné agus Inniu (1994)

Seal i Neipeal (2004)

Pianó Mhín na bPréachán (2011)

Teach an Gheafta (2018)

PLAYS

Oíche Dhrochghealaí (2005)

Mairimid Leis na Mistéirí: Trí ghearrdhrámaí (2006)

Where the Curlews Cry (2018)

WRITING IN ENGLISH

Caiseal na gCorr (2002)

Light on Distant Hills: A Memoir (2009)

Soul Space: A Book of Spiritual Wisdom (2014)

The View From the Glen: Selected Prose (2018)

CONTENTS

AN tEARAGAIL: RÉAMHRÁ

Cathal Ó Searcaigh

Tá cónaí orm i Mín an Leá faoi scáth an Earagail. Tá an sliabh uasal, uaibhreach seo i gcónaí i gcúl m'aigne. Tá sé de shíor á shíneadh féin isteach i mo shamhlaíocht agus i mo shaothar. Amanta bhéarfainn mionna gur ar Fujiyama na Seapáine atá mé ag amharc. Chan gan fáth a deirim sin nó tá déanamh agus dealramh, crot agus cosúlacht an Earagail ar aon chuma lena bhráthair sa tSeapáin. Tá maorgacht dhiamhair, bheannaithe ag baint leo beirt, rud a fhágann go bhfuil áit lárnach acu i saol agus i saoithiúlacht na ndaoine atá ina gcónaí ag a mbun. Nuair a bhí m'athair féin anonn i mblianta agus an aois ag titim go trom air, shamhlaigh sé go raibh an tEaragail ag teacht anuas le seilbh a ghlacadh air. Tá mé féin amhlaidh. Tá mé faoi gheasa ag an Earagail.

Is é mo mhian i gcónaí a ghabháil amach, bíodh an lá maith nó olc, faoi ghrian, faoi ghaoth nó faoi gharbhshíon agus siúlóid bheag sléibhe a dhéanamh i gcomharsanacht an Earagail. Is aoibhinn liom suí i gclúideanna scoite uaigneacha i mbrollach na gcnoc nó seasamh ar dhroimeanna deasa fraoigh amuigh ar an réiteach ag amharc uaim ar áilleacht na tíre ó shliabh go muir. Ní iarrfainn a mhalairt ach a bheith amuigh i bhfairsingeacht na gcnoc agus na gcaorán. Seo mo thearmann anama, m'aireagal sóláis.

Is doiligh an tEaragail a cheapadh i bhfocla. Ard! Starránach! Maorga! Is cuma cé na haidiachtaí a mbainim úsáid astu, níl siad ábalta an sliabh seo a thabhairt chun léire is chun solais mar ba mhian liom. Má deirim go bhfuil sé níos gile ná an t-airgead geal, níos goirme ná uisce fómhair, níl ansin ach lagchuntas ar raon dathanna an tsléibhe. Na healaíontóirí seo a bhfuil bua na péintéireachta acu tá sé d'éirim acusan an tEaragail a cheapadh go beo, beacht, soiléir, cé acu ar canbhás, in uiscedhath nó i líníocht. Chan iontas domh a bheith in éad leo nó is tréitheach an ealaín atá acu. Faraor, níl agamsa ach friotal gonta an fhocail leis an ghnó seo a dhéanamh.

Amuigh i bhfairsingeacht an tsléibhe is minic a mhothaím síocháin an Domhnaigh sna háiteacha a mbím ag siúl ach fosta cumhaidh na beatha. Tá go leor de bhailte beaga na mbunchnoc bánaithe; domasach na gcuibhreann ag tiompú aríst ina shliabh ar an Dúnán, i Mín na gCapóg, i bProchlais agus i Mín na bPoll. Iadsan a thug nádúr fiáin na domasaí seo chun míne shíl siad, is dócha, go raibh síoraíocht ina gcuid oibre. Sna bailte fearainn seo faoi scáth an Earagail chonaic mé i m'am féin na daoine deireanacha, mná agus fir nár phós ariamh is nach raibh clann ina ndiaidh, ag gabháil ón tsaol go huaigneach. A ndálta siúd, iarmharán atá ionam féin fosta, an t-aon duine de bhunadh Mhín an Leá atá fágtha ar an bhaile anois. Do bheatha na haigne a thug mé toil seachas do phórú na clainne.

I dtaca leis an Earagail níl lá dá n-éiríonn nach bhfuil mé ag déanamh iontais dó; a chló is a chrot ó shéasúr go séasúr is ó sholas go solas. Amanta tá sé chomh dúr le tuairnín na mbrúitín mar a déarfadh an seandream. Amanta eile tá sé lasta faoi aoibh na bhflaitheas le luí na gréine.

Tá buanaíocht aige sa tsaol nach bhfuil ag an duine. Is fada an lá agus is cian ó saolaíodh é as broinn deargtha na Giniúna. Mhothaigh sé lena ré teas tréamanta agus fuacht oighearleice. I bhfad siar chonaic sé an duine ag

teacht i dtír is i dtreis ar sholáthar seilge is ar chnas-
ach cladaigh. D'fhéach sé ar lomadh is ar loisceadh na
ngarbhchríocha faoina scáth is an duine á dtabhairt
chun míntíreachais. Chonaic sé a dtáinig is tchífidh
sé a dtiocfaidh. Go ndéanfar dhá leath den domhan
buanóidh sé ag ceann ár nGleanna ag breathnú uaidh
ar theacht is ar imeacht an duine.

Le gach píosa próis dá bhfuil anseo, le gach dán,
ba mhaith liom léaró beag solais a chaitheamh ar an
Earagail as an tuigbheáil a tháinig chugam den tsliabh
i ndiaidh na mblianta de thriallta ina thimpeall, á
bhreathnú is á mhóradh.

— II —

Ag amharc uait de shíor
ar thimthriall an tsaoil
ní chuireann ár mbeatha uafás ort,
ní chuireann ár mbás áthas ort.

Ní hionann tú agus muidinne,
na neacha eaglacha
a dhéanann an saol a thomhas i laethanta,
déanann tusa an saol a thomhas i gclocha.

Chan iontas ar bith go bhfuil diamhaireacht ag baint leis an Earagail nó tá cuisle na grianchloiche le feiceáil go soiléir i ndéanamh agus i ndealramh an tsléibhe. Bhíothas ariamh anall den bharúil go raibh cumhacht as an choitiantacht ag cuisliú sa chloch seo. Mheas ár ndaoine romhainn go raibh foinse feasa agus fuinnimh ag sní i ngráinníní na cloiche agus go bhféadfaí an chumhacht seo a chur i bhfearas agus i bhfónamh dá mbeatha, dá sláinte anama agus coirp ach scealpóg bheag den chloch a bheith ar iompar leo.

Bhí mo mháthair féin lánchinnte d'éirim dhiamhair na cloiche agus thaiscigh sí píosaí den rúnchloch seo timpeall an tí le muid a thabhairt slán as gach baol agus breoiteacht. D'fhágfadh sí píosaí amuigh fá na cuibhrinn fosta le cur le taca is le tiubh na talún. Agus mé i mo dhéagóir baothdhána is minic a chuaigh mé go bog is go cruaidh uirthi á bréagnú is ag rá léithe gur ag déanamh mínóis a bhí sí. Ach níor baineadh dá cothrom ariamh í le díomas mo chuid cainte. Bhí sí diongbháilte ina creideamh féin in orthaí, i ngeasrógaí, agus san aos sí. Glacaim leis anois go raibh ciall fheasach aici do nithe agus do neacha nach dtig faoi dhlínse na tuigbheála.

— III —

Bhí sí den bharúil gur beag ár gcumhacht thar ár gcinniúint ach chreid sí go raibh orthaí ann agus clocha bua a bhéarfadh díonaíocht dúinn ón anachain. Anois agus mé anonn i mblianta tá mé den bharúil chéanna mé féin. Is annamh a théim chun siúil gan mo chuid orthaí cosanta a bheith in éineacht liom. Orthu siúd bíonn scealp bheag grianchloiche á hiompar liom i dtólamh.

Sliabh na grianchloiche. Sliabh na gile. Sliabh na Glóire. Sin an tEaragail. Chan iontas ar bith go bhfuil tarraingt na ndaoine air. Tá muid faoi gheasa aige.

Ar na mallaibh agus mé ag scríobh in am mharbh na hoíche, mar a bhím de ghnách, chuala mé rothlú tobann torannach sa spéir i dtreo an Earagail. Amach liom láithreach le tréan fiosrachta. Iontas na n-iontas bhí an tEaragail lasta suas go taibhsiúil faoi bhéim solais agus héileacaptar ag timpeallú an tsléibhe. Ba léir domh ansin go raibh duine inteacht caillte agus gur feachtas tarrthála a bhí ar siúl ar an tsliabh.

Chaith mé amuigh is istigh ar uair an chloig ag amharc ar an dianchuardach seo ó m'fhuinneog bhairr; na bíomaí móra solais ag siúl an tsléibhe go maorga, á ghealadh is á ghrinniú.

Shamhlófá gur slua aingeal nó neacha glémhaiseacha éigin ó chríocha uachtaracha na spéire a thuirling ar an tsliabh. Agus cá bhfios nach bhfuil an tsamhailt sin i bhfad ón fhírinne. Lá arna mhárach fuair mé amach gur "Mylie Naofa", mar a tugadh air go háitiúil, a bhásaigh ar an tsliabh.

Chaith Maolmhuire Ó Gallachóir bunús a shaoil ag siúl ar shlí an tSoiscéil. Bhí cead agus beannacht na hEaglaise aige le bheith ina dhíseartach. Ní shílim go raibh méin an uaignis ann i ndáiríre lena bheatha a chaitheamh ar leataobh óna chomhdhaoine. Thaitin comhluadar agus cuideachta leis. Chónaigh sé ina theach féin ar an Bhealtaine agus mhair sé mar bhall den phobal, a shaol á thabhairt aige go huile don bheatha chrábhaidh agus do shlánú an anama.

Is beag riachtanais bheatha a bhí uaidh. Rinne daoine déirce air i dtaca le bia agus éadach. Bhí a bheatha ag teacht ó Neamh chuige, a dúirt sé liom uair amháin. Is minic a bheannaigh sé isteach chugam agus é amuigh ag déanamh a thráthanna crábhaidh. Chuaigh a aigne ghrinn, íogair, ghníomhach i bhfeidhm orm agus cé gurbh annamh muid ar chomhthuigbheáil ar chúrsaí creidimh agus cráifeachta níor thóg sin ariamh an focal garbh ná an focal maslach eadrainn. Bhí sé intuigthe againn beirt go raibh cead aighnis againn sna comhráití seo agus chuir sin fiúr spreagúil ar an chaint.

— IV —

Bhí meas agam ar Mylie agus an bealach a roghnaigh sé dó féin. Tá sé doiligh éalú ó chuing an tsaoil, na bacanna sóisialta a shárú, laincisí teaghlaigh a scaoileadh. Rinne Mylie é sin. Thug sé móidghealladh cráifeachta agus choinnigh sé é. An saol a ghlac sé air féin ní raibh sé furasta. Ach lean sé an ród a bhí lena mhian. Bhí a shúil ar an bheatha shíoraí seachas ar an bheatha shaolta.

Mo dhálta féin bhí sé tugtha don choisíocht; an siúl mar shlí machnaimh. Uair sa bhliain bhí sé de chleachtadh aige turas na gcnoc a dhéanamh ón Mhucais trasna na hAchlaí go barr an Earagail. Oilithreacht bhliantúil. Mhothaigh sé agus é ag guí ar bharr na gcnoc go raibh sé níos cóngaraí do ghrásta Dé agus d'áras na naomh. Is minic a dúirt sé sin liom. Ní raibh áit ní b'fhearr leis le síothlú ón tsaol, a déarfadh sé, ná ar bharr cnoic. In ainneoin go raibh sé deich mbliana agus ceithre scór bhí spreagadh ann go fóill leis an Earagail a dhreapadh. Ansiúd ar mhalaidh an tsléibhe d'imigh an dé deiridh as. Fuarthas a chorp le teacht an lae. Shocraigh Mylie, measaim féin, gur ar an Earagail a bheadh fód a bháis agus fuair sé a iarraidh.

Cuimhneoidh mé i gcónaí ar an oíche úd agus an tEaragail lasta suas ar dhóigh nach bhfaca mé ariamh amhail is go raibh searmanas diaga éigin á cheiliúradh ar mhaithe le Mylie. Fuair sé bás mar a d'fhóir dó agus é ag dreapadh i dtreo na Glóire.

Cúpla bliain ó shin, mar fhreagra ar Mylie nuair a d'fhiafraigh sé domh an raibh creideamh ar bith agam i ndáiríre, tháinig na véarsaí seo liom tráthnóna amháin samhraidh agus an tír faoi sholas.

ADHRADH NA NDÚL

Níl d'adhradh a dhíth
ach a bheith lúcháireach
i láthair an tSolais seo
a spréann a thíolacthaí
anseo i measc na mbeo.

Níl d'adhradh a dhíth
ach na blátha seo a mhóradh,
a gcumhracht a cheiliúradh,
ligint do naomhluan a ngile
an croí a shoilsiú.

Níl d'adhradh a dhíth
ach seasamh ag an gheafta seo
agus glacadh go buíoch
le naomhshacraimint na gealaí
agus le beannachtaí na gaoithe.

— VI —

Tá Mary ar shlí na fírinne anois ach nach é sin an tslí a shiúil sí agus í ina beatha; slí a bhí umhal, múinte, uchtúil. Slí na fírinne! Mar dhuine, bhí sí dílis ariamh dá dúchas féin agus dá dúchas Dhún Lúicheach.

Do Mhary, ba é Dún Lúiche an teallach, an tobar agus an tearmann.

Ba sa spás scóipiúil sléibhe sin a d'ap a haigne. B'ann a d'fhás sí i dtreo an tsolais. Dúirt sí féin gur láidrigh Dún Lúiche í; gur ansin a fuair sí an acmhainn is an neart leis an ailse a bhí ag siúl léithe a iompar go cróga.

Nuair a bhí sí ina girseach i nDún Lúiche bhí cleachtadh aici a bheith ag cur i gcoinne bristeacha borba gaoithe agus í ar a bealach na bhaile ón scoil; gaoth ghéar gharbhshíne na gcnoc anuas ó Shliabh Sneachta.

Tuigeadh dithe agus í ag teacht i méadaíocht i nDún Lúiche nach raibh, is nach mbeadh, an saol ariamh réidh, simplí, gan stró. Ach mar a dúirt sí liom uair amháin, d'ullmhaigh an tEaragail í le seasamh ar a cosa féin is a haghaidh a thabhairt ar an tsaol go dearfach.

Anois tá Cor Úr curtha ina cinniúint.

Tá an saol fágtha ina diaidh aici agus í imithe uainn ar bhealach na nglún, ar bhealach na rún. Tá sí imithe uainn amach bealach an tsléibhe chun na Síoraíochta, a bealach féin chun an bhaile.

Léifidh mé dán ar a dtugtar "Cor Úr" lenár gcara ionúin, Mary Murray, a thionlacan ar chúrsa buan na Cinniúna.

PREFACE

Patrick Breslin

I was eleven when I first saw Errigal, the highest mountain in Ireland's County Donegal, but I already knew I wouldn't climb its steep, sea-facing slope. "It's all scree", my father said. I may have been the only child in the mid-twentieth century South Bronx who knew the word scree.

My father worked the graveyard shift in a hospital on the edge of Greenwich Village, then rode the subway home to breakfast and rest. In those quick years between the onset of language and primary school's reboot of the immigrant's child, I would sit beside him for bedtime stories of his childhood in Donegal; sessions that ended sideways, the parent dropping off to sleep, the child rising to dim the light.

Like darkroom chemicals, those stories fixed images in my mind: blue and orange horse-drawn carts on narrow lanes, dark drystone fences framing green fields, leafy potato plants in long drills, communal meals on the bog where sodden slabs of turf were sliced and stood on end to dry and shrink in the insistent winds, the sea and the dunes where you collected marram grass to rethatch the roofs, water drawn from wells, milk from the few cows on every small farm, boys roaming the countryside playing tricks on stern farmers, old women in black skirts and shawls. And looming above it all, Errigal, the great mountain.

At eleven those images came alive for me. Both my parents were native Irish-speakers, born in the parish of Cloughaneely and raised on neighboring small farms on rocky soil between Errigal and the sea, farms that produced few crops but many children. My father was the youngest of fourteen, my mother had eight siblings. The oldest male inherited the farm. Most of the others left for migrant work. Letterkenny was the nearest town of any size. In its square, down from the church, fathers would hire their children out as servants to prosperous Protestant farmers from the Lagan, the rich agricultural land between there and Derry. The year my mother was hired out, she ran away after two days and walked home, thirty miles or more. Errigal would have shown her the way.

Whatever drove her to break her father's pledge, he didn't send her back.

Most young men left for summer farm work in Scotland once the potatoes were planted at home. My father did that through the First World War, the 1916 Easter Rising and the Spanish flu that caught him on a boat to Glasgow, killed several of his mates but spared him. Eventually, the promise of better work drew him to New York in 1927. My mother had emigrated a couple of years earlier. They met and married during the Great Depression, began a family during World War II, events that suspended Donegal as if in amber for a quarter-century. In 1951, when they returned with my brother and me for a summer-long visit, it was still to the world my father had described: no electricity outside the towns, no plumbing in the farmhouses, turf fires for heat and cooking.

So vivid were my father's stories that I tried to replicate one my first morning in Donegal – shinnying down the tree outside the second floor bedroom that had let him slip out to join his friends on summer nights. I opened the window and leaned out, to confront the reality that trees grow thick and wide in forty years. The slender trunk my father had wrapped his arms and legs around was now massive, no handhold. I had the sense to abandon the plan before I broke my neck.

We didn't attempt Errigal that trip. The steep north face that rose just up the road from us was the side covered with loose stones and splintered quartzite, avalanches waiting to happen, my father's scree. The trailhead for the safer back slope was a half day's walk away. My parents were more intent on seeing friends and relatives, who were legion. They bought me a used bicycle soon after we arrived and I spent summer days riding every road for miles around. No one worried about traffic – we knew of only one car in the parish – nor about my getting lost since turning towards Errigal would take me home. The rising road to my father's house pointed directly at its dramatic peak.

But even though we didn't climb it, Errigal was my first mountain. To that point, the tallest thing I'd seen was the Empire State Building, an obelisk stretching above the distant cluster of Manhattan skyscrapers visible from a hall window outside our fourth-floor apartment. Errigal was just up the road, and twice as tall.

Every child should have a mountain. It affects the way you think, the way you learn. Trees age and topple, land erodes, rivers change course, events that can be witnessed in the space of a human lifetime, or less. Mountains more than any other feature on the landscape seem eternal, and when we contemplate them, we're encouraged to think about long spans of time – centuries, millennia, or the hundreds of millions of years of geologic time.

Roving on my bicycle that summer, I gathered my own Cloughaneely memories: the incessant sea winds that somehow were never at my back, no matter my direction; an aunt angrily chasing the two chickens I'd liberated after she'd locked them in a shed in preparation for Sunday dinner; the kindly women who would wave me down as I passed their small houses, explain how they were related to me and on which side, if not both, and invite me in for tea and toast with jam and hard-boiled eggs; the cows and pigs and chickens and geese; the carts I passed, top-heavy with turf from the bog; a wake for a young woman the night we arrived, the first dead person I remember seeing; another night staring into the crumbling red embers of the fire beside the death bed of Neil Duffy, one of the best-known shanachies of Ireland, while my father paid respects; sent up the hill to bring down the cows for water and the noon milking and, knowing nothing of cows but cowboy movies, stampeding them and their swollen udders past my mother's house in a cloud of dust while she begged her brother not to kill me.

Two memories revealed my parents' contrasting connection to Ireland, although I didn't understand it then: my mother in her dress trimmed in red, hair permed, the stylish visitor from America standing out from the women of the parish; my father, so blended into a group of men in tweed jackets and caps smoking and chatting on a bench against the wall of a neighboring house that I didn't recognise him until I was almost beside them.

All those memories are framed by the Donegal landscape, Errigal always somewhere in the scene, as Mount Fuji in central Japan is in Katsushika Hokusai's *Thirty-Six Views*. As in my own childhood memories, the mountain itself dominates only a few of Hokusai's woodblock prints. Most show human activity: farmers, merchants, carpenters, coopers, fishermen and woodsmen going about their tasks, soldiers and monks on their journeys. But always, somewhere in the background, stands Fuji, a silent, eternal witness. Can his meaning be any other than the fleeting nature of human life, human work, ambitions, desires, energy, compared with the hundreds of millions of years' perspective of the mountain?

As a child, I was decades away from posing such questions. But I definitely noticed my mountain. Like Fuji, Errigal, thanks to its prominence and its shape, is an iconic presence on the landscape. At 2,464 feet, it is only one-fifth Fuji's height, and 34 mountains in Ireland are taller (although not by much; a mere 286 feet and Errigal's in the top ten.) But Errigal, like Fuji, has prominence. It stands out from other mountains.

Prominence is not just a visual impression. You can measure it quite precisely by the fine contour lines that show elevation on a topographic map. Every peak has a contour line around its summit. Each drop to lower elevation is marked by another line, according to the map's scale. The distance from the peak to the lowest contour line that encircles it without including another peak is the mountain's prominence. Errigal's is 2,257 feet. It's almost all prominence.

It's also cone shaped. The tops of most Irish mountains, even the highest ones, were sanded round or shaved into long ridges by glacier ice over thousands of years. Errigal's sharp, sky-piercing summit is a nunatak, a peak that stood above glaciers during recent ice ages and so escaped the grinding of their recession.

My parents gave me many gifts, including a college education, uncommon in those years for someone growing up in the South Bronx. But now I think that trip to Donegal at age eleven, and my father's stories that set the scene for it, were equally important. They made Errigal, and surrounding Cloughaneely, as integral a part of my childhood as the South Bronx streets, and ever since, they've drawn me back at every opportunity.

By the time I was next in Ireland, in 1960, electricity and running water had reached the parish's farmhouses. Where bicycles had whispered down the roads, now occasional cars roared by the small houses and their headlights raked the hillsides at night. Profound cultural changes were underway. People stopped meeting with their buckets or animals at the crossroads spring in Baltony. Electricity brought light, then television. Soon, the benches outside houses where people had gathered for craic on summer evenings, and the shanachies spinning stories in rooms lit by lanterns and fireplace flames, gave way to ghostly cathode-ray flickers on the darkened windows.

On succeeding trips, I continued exploring, excavating my way down towards the bedrock of family and history. At the same time, I would later learn, a burst of geological research was taking a longer view – revealing the four hundred million-year-old history of Donegal's landscape. The first studies of Donegal geology came in the 1830s, around the time Hokusai was doing his woodblocks. But it was only in the second half of the twentieth century that systematic research traced how some of the most cataclysmic events in the history of the planet played out in Donegal. Eventually, I would find myself weaving my own sense of Cloughaneely roots into that immeasurably longer history.

Geologists divide Earth's four and a half billion years into 22 periods. Some five hundred million years ago, in the Cambrian Period, life on Earth exploded from single cell organisms into a vast profusion of complex forms. Roughly a hundred million years later,

in the Devonian, two continents, tectonic plates floating on the Earth's ductile mantle like huge barges that
have slipped their moorings, collided to fuse the super
continent, Pangea. Vast land masses tilted steeply sky-
ward, and magna spewed from deep in the Earth's core
to form rock on the surface. In Donegal, the upheaval
formed the Derryveagh Mountains along a southwest
to northeast line known as the Gweebara Fault whose
local features today are the narrow valley and lake
of Glenveagh National Park, Errigal, the granite and
quartzite colossus, and in the mountain's shadow, the
Poisoned Glen, lately a popular site for rock-climbing,
but wild and lonely when I first ventured into it.

Once, walking through there on a cold, misty day,
the thought that "my feet know this ground" suddenly
formed in my mind. I'd never had such a sense before,
nor since. But the Poisoned Glen is a strange place,
even the origin of its name shrouded in history and
myth. One version of the Balor legend, about an evil
Cyclops who pirated from nearby Tory Island, says
his blood contaminated the land in the glen when, in
accordance with a prophecy, the grandson he'd failed
to murder as an infant thrust a sword through his
single eye. A more prosaic explanation is splurge, a
plant that grows there and sickens livestock. Or it
could be that a British cartographer, one of several
colonial agents dispatched to Ireland in the 1830s to

supplant Irish place names with English equivalents, was simply careless.

All these features of the landscape, and their associations, were the backdrop to my amateur attempts to trace my ancestry. I could picture my people in concrete settings. I learned for example that one grandfather came from the other side of the Derryeaghs, and on weekends walked some twenty miles each way through the mountains to court my grandmother, eventually winning a wife, a farm, and a position as the local schoolteacher.

Gradually, rocks themselves – inescapable in Cloughaneely – became the focus of my curiosity. The parish name itself refers to a specific rock central to the Balor story: a white granite boulder mounted on a plinth outside the town of Falcarragh is said to be the rock on which Balor cleaved the head from his enemy, the chieftain Macaneely, who had fathered the boy who would eventually slay Balor.

In 1978, I discovered rocks closer to family history when I went with my father to see something he'd built as a young man. If you want to feel rooted in a place, rest your back against a massive drystone wall erected by your father's hands half a century before, and reflect that many of its stones emerged molten from the Earth's mantle millions of years before that. And that some ten to fifteen thousand years ago, receding glaciers likely left those stones, like a building supply store delivery, on the land that would become his family's farm.

At the end of a field behind the house where he was born and grew up there's a gate to the lower fields and a path wide enough for a horse-drawn wagon or a tractor. The field beside it, on higher ground, is held in place by the wall he built when he spent the summer of 1924 at home instead of doing seasonal work in Scotland. It's 10 feet high most of its 30 foot length. The rocks, different sizes and shapes, fit together like a jigsaw puzzle, no mortar. Now, almost a century later, not one has fallen out of place. I recalled once driving with my father past farms in upstate New York and pointing to rows of tumbled down stones around the pastures. I called them walls. "They were never walls", he scoffed. "Just piles of rocks."

Donegal's rocks, which are found in surprising places, tell geologists a second great story about the Earth's history – continental drift. The history of the area, and of my family, is filled with departures. At least half of both my parents' families left Errigal behind when they crossed over to America, the same journey made by millions more from all over Ireland. But long before its people departed, an entire continent left the mountain behind.

Pangea lasted a million years or so before the restless Earth shifted again. This time, part of the super continent split off and began to drift westwards, the widening gap would eventually become the Atlantic Ocean. In fact the gap is still widening. When I flew to Ireland this year, I traveled over an Atlantic Ocean roughly four meters wider than the one my parents crossed when they left Ireland for America in the 1920s. The reason is churning in the Earth's mantle, sending heat currents and material to the surface, spreading the sea floor, the mechanism that drives continental drift.

For hundreds of millions of years, the Atlantic's sea floor has been spreading a few centimeters a year. Some of the rocks that first tumbled down Errigal's slopes 400 million years ago are now in Eastern Canada.

These findings generate an irresistible image: Errigal the silent witness to the departure of both the land around it over millions of years, and the sons and daughters of its slopes in recent centuries. While I dug into family separations and migrations, teams of geologists deciphered the planet's history in Donegal's rocks, finding evidence for similar processes on the scale of continents. At one time Errigal gazed down on what is now North America, and then watched it drift away.

Our world today teems with uprooted people — immigrants and refugees set in motion by war, famine, exploitation of forests and water, separated from their land, from the horizon they'd grown up within, the line of mountains in the distance or the shape of the sea coast stretching into the mists. All that lost to them now, leaving the inner person lost as well. Where do I belong? Where can I settle? What bargain must I strike to survive? What's different today is the scale. The process itself is as old as history. The earliest chapters of the Bible tell us that: Adam and Eve cast out, Cain cast out, the Jews cast out. And their children assimilate.

In a mid-century South Bronx tenement, my father dealt with that loss by passing on his memories to his children. He gave me, and a bit later my brother, a sense of connection to a corner of Donegal. Historically, that has not been typical for first-generation Americans. The incentive, the need, was to assimilate. In our case, my mother saw to that. My father's role was more subversive. Perhaps he was just indulging his own nostalgia. But in any case, he gave me a second country where I feel at home, where the land is familiar to my feet.

And when he was 82, I was able to give him something back: finally, a hike together up Errigal's back slope. It was the year after my mother died, after ten years of mental and physical decline. Caring for her day and night had revealed his devotion and taken fifty pounds off his robust frame, leaving him all bones and craggy features, like a rock outcropping himself, although still strong and active.

I expected a fairly easy stroll, but Errigal rises out of vast soggy boglands covered by ground-hugging, boot-snagging heather and veined by iodine-tinctured streams you ford or leap to reach the first real incline. I could feel the effort by the time I got there, but my father was ten yards ahead and moving steadily up the switchback trail through shattered granite scree. Hundreds of feet higher up he stopped and waited for me by a circle of stones that from below looked to be at the peak. But as I came up to him, I could see the trail continuing along a narrow ridge leading to two summits, patches of snow just below them.

"Can't you hurry a bit?" he asked. "Do you want it to get around that your old man beat you to the top of Errigal?"

I remember wanting a rest, but a cold wind off the sea was scouring the mountain's flanks and my father resumed his steady tramp. Ten minutes more took us up the ridge to the first summit, down into a saddle, and up again to the high peak, where we braced ourselves against the wind and took in the vast sweep of the country dropping away from us. I remember sunlight had broken through and looking out to the turbulent North Atlantic we could see white dots of houses on Inishboffin and beyond on far Tory. To our left, the length of Dunlewy Lake, dark blue in the bright sun; to our right, the Altan lakes set like jewels on the bosom of Aghla Mountain, below us, past the jumble of scree, the whole parish of Cloughaneely spread out. If my gift to him was the climb near the end of his life, his to me was all the world I was seeing from Errigal's peak, the world he'd made part of mine.

Washington, D.C.

ERRIGAL:
A SACRED MOUNTAIN

All of my life I have lived under this spectacular mountain but however much I see and appraise it, it never loses its mystique for me.

It has an uncanny hold over my mind and my imagination, a strange fascination that keeps me attentive to its inscrutable presence.

Standing there ancient and solitary in its scarred grey magnificence, vagrant shadows hovering above its head, it seems to me to be much more than its earth and its rocks.

It could well be the seat of divinities.

Despite our wet, hill weather which often obscures it in cloudy vapours, and overcast days with only fitful glimpses of the sun to lighten its blunt face, I'm compelled out by its mesmeric pull to view it everyday.

Errigal has many faces. From Mín an Leá where I see it daily it is a shapely cone of grey. The most iconic representations of it are from this side. It's this north-facing, pyramid-shaped, commanding presence that attracts painters and photographers. From other vantage points, from Gaoth Dobhair, for instance, or from Gleann Bheithe, it is still a stately sight but more humped and jagged in its appearance. A stout benign Ancient.

Our perspective of Errigal is often shaped by its colour, which varies, depending on flourishes and fluctuations of light, from rose pink to ivory; from a hazy blue to a glaze of purple. On an evening of flaming sunset it can be a florid red or in a fall of fresh snow it becomes a dazzling spectacle of white like something conjured from the Other-World.

Although I have climbed Errigal many times in my impetuous younger days, I'm inclined now, in my more mature years, to circle round its flanks. A reverential walk, you might say, in homage to its presence.

I have shifted from the sense of ascendancy I got when I climbed it in my youth to a feeling of awe and humility when I view it now from below; a feeling, no doubt, chastened by the realisation of its fragility.

While it watches over us and enhances our lives with its graceful presence, we have a duty to respect and protect it. It can no longer, of its own nature, withstand the crunch and the grinding down; the stress and the pressure of the heavy football it has endured in recent years.

However I'm glad to say that a genuine effort is being made at present to protect the mountain; an environmentally friendly approach that maintains it, and yet, manages to give access to all those who wish to climb it.

As for myself, I will always pay tribute to it from my window of wonder in Mín an Leá and I will follow my own pilgrim path around it, genuflecting and giving thanks to its enduring and sovereign glory.

I think of Mount Kailos in Tibet, a Buddhist and a Hindu sacred site, where the observance of the pilgrimage does not involve climbing to the top but ritually circling it, most often, on one's hands and knees. In fact it's forbidden for anyone to ever stand on the sacred summit. In the minds of its devotees it would be an outrage, an act of utter desecration to climb the mountain, and thus, violate the sanctity of its guardian deity.

I'm not suggesting that people should stop climbing Errigal but rather, that they approach and ascend it with a certain dignity, a little decorum at least, as befits an Oratory; the sacred space that in Irish is known as an tAireagal.

— 2 —

Despite its lofty eminence and its felt presence, it has no lore, no preserved past in any of our annals. Until recent times it stood alone in unwritten anonymity.

How strange! I wonder what the first people who settled on these coastal headlands more than five thousand years ago called this spectacular presence that dominated their landscape.

I cannot believe that it was nameless in those far-off eras of antiquity. Our distant ancestry must have been as conscious of it as we are today.

Whatever its ancient name was it did not survive the vagaries of Time. Christianity annexed it to its own beliefs and renamed it An tAireagal. Aireagal/Earagail means Oratory, a small chapel or a place of private worship.

Brian Lacey, a distinguished archaeologist and historian who now lives in Dún Lúiche, has made much of the survival, and as yet, the heightened sense of a Lugh mythos here in our local area. Lugh was a Celtic deity much revered on the mainland of Europe as well as in Ireland.

The intense concentration of Lugh lore here in Cloich Cheann Fhaola, carried down to us in the racial memory of our people recalls, perhaps, a time in the far past, as Brian Lacey suggests, when this area was a locus for Lugh worship.

In this setting, Errigal, our dominant peak, may have been Sliabh Lugh, a mountain devoted to the deity; a venerated and a ritual site that sanctified the surrounding landscape and its people in the name of Lugh.

This ancient belief, a heady Earth worship with its fiery mixture of spirit, superstition and sorcery would have been an unholy allegiance and a threat to the spreading Christian faith. They stamped it out, or else, shaped it anew in the light of their own beliefs. Sliabh Lugh became Errigal, converted to the new dispensation by a subtle change of name.

I'm sure it did not move easily from one developed faith to the more dominant one. But I like to think that whatever the changes brought about in appeal and in attitude by this cult-shift, it did not diminish the mountain's standing as a place of power, a sanctum of Earth-energy.

And it's still there. That spirited power persists in the mountain. An intensity that quickens the heart and enlivens the mind of all those who attune themselves to it.

Although I liken it sometimes to the mystical Mount Mera of Hindu scripture, Errigal, however, is not hidden away on some astral plane of unknowingness. It is a solid, terrestrial actuality; an upthrust of earth and glinting quartzite; a witnessing presence to our fleeting lives.

In the morning, awakening sometimes, to a pristine view of the mountain from my upstairs window, I see it sitting there in a posture of calm contemplation like one of the many sculptured Buddhas I have about the house.

Even on wet grey days when it's shrouded in rainclouds, I still feel its presence, its power. It's always there, watchful, essential, salutary, a part of what I am.

— 3 —

I have always been drawn to Errigal, in no small part because my grandfather, Joe Sharkey, came from An Dúnán, a townland tucked away in a little fold at the foot of the mountain.

In a sense, my kinship with my grandfather's people strengthened my bond with Errigal. As a child I was often up there visiting them. At that time An Dúnán had three households and they were all Sharkeys. Hill farmers, they were the sole occupants of the place. Each farmstead was a neat acreage of tillage and pasture. Each had a flock of sheep that grazed the mountain.

At home we called them "Muintir an Eargail", Errigal people, on account of their closeness to it. In my child's mind all of my An Dúnan kin were living embodiments of the mountain. It seemed to me then that the mountain, in true grandeur, rose sheer out of their lives.

When they themselves talked about Errigal, it usually concerned its changing weathers and how that impeded or benefited their day-to-day labours. In fact they were as much a part of the mountain as the comings and goings of the seasonal vegation that flourished around it.

My grandfather told me that the dip at the top of Errigal was scooped out by Noah's Ark, when, by mischance, it was put off course at night in a strong gale and it struck the mountain. He had the story on good authority, he said, from a learned man, "a fear foghlamtha", who treated him to a "wee drop" in a local pub. My grandfather's most fanciful stories always had a whiff of whiskey about them.

Errigal, whether it's wrapped in a cashmere of cloud or wearing a shimmering negligee of snow is forever, a witnessing presence to our fleeting lives. My father towards the end of his life believed that the mountain was coming down to take him away.

"Tán tEargal ag teacht fá mo choinne," he'd say as if he were expecting a friend with a vehicle to take him on a roadtrip.

— 4 —

I like walking, taking to the paths and the tracks around Errigal without a mapped-out strategy, just a giddy itinerary of aimlessness.

Off course I'm privileged to have a certain amount of leisured freedom to indulge in this delightful vagabondage.

A path is the imprint of human history on the landscape.

I become absorbed in their topographies, their ups and downs, their restless meanderings, their stubbornness.

I want to know about their flora and fauna, their geological heritage, their human lineage.

I like to think of these old paths as being patrician, the aged lineaments of the landscape.

I'm not writing a trail guide to steer you around Errigal but more a literary companion to hearten your walks and to encourage you to engage with the mountain, not merely as another peak to be climbed, but rather as a presence to be contemplated.

Although I'm not following a pilgrim path or doing prostrations around the mountain, I hope that these reflective walks bring some merit other than foot sores and swellings. I hope they keep the Spirit up.

Errigal has a way of touching us that is given to few mountains. Often it makes the heart stand still in wonder, as it were, while watching shifts of light across its face and a heightening of its colour. On these occasions it glows with an immense intensity as if some Revelation was at hand.

This mystic appeal is what keeps me attentive to Errigal.

I love journeys; mystery tours; rambles. Every evening I take my mind out for a jaunt in the mountains and the moors around Errigal. Even a long walk around the table can be awe-inspiring. It can be an outing in the imagination. If you can't go on a journey you can always take a sight seeing tour of the Self. There are more things in the heaven and the Earth of our minds than we know of.

To benefit from a journey you have to cultivate a sense of awareness, a sense of openess, a readiness to experience whatever the journey brings forth.

I remember my old friend Maggie Neddie Donnchaidh, my next door neighbour here in Mín an Leá, a woman who never left her home except once in her lifetime; a long epic journey to West Clare on a June day in 1963. And back home again on the self-same day. Her sister Biddy was married to a Clare man and they lived in London. That year they decided to spend a holiday with his relations in County Clare and Maggie was invited to visit them. She did but it was a flying visit. She hired a local driver, Charlie John Óig, one of the few locals to have a car at that time, to drive her there and back on the same day. From that day onwards, her favourite topic of conversation was "The day I went to County Clare" she would describe every detail of that trip; the people she met and the places that she saw. Every twist and turn, every snatch and scrap of conversation. She remembered everything; what she had seen, what she heard and what she had felt.

Years later, when I told her of my adventures while travelling in Europe or in America, her innocent face would light up and she'd say "Well isn't that strange. That's exactly like what happened to me the day I went to Co Clare." And that was her off on her journey of wonder once more. As she got older, this one-day Odyssey became more magical and more epical. She kept reinventing it, renewing it. She made a spirited connection with her vital creative energies on that journey. The journey restored her, enriched to the real world of her everyday life.

Her only journey became all journeys. She found a space to move in with her whole body, her whole mind. She became attentive, and attuned to the sights and sounds of eye and ear. She became a Seer — a *file*, a poet.

Maggie Neddie Dhonnchaidh is dead for many years now but her one-day, Homeric journey continues to reverberate in my mind; a shining epic that reveals the world of the ordinary, conceals the marvellous. Maggie's story brought to light for me the momentousness of the ordinary.

Going out to walk is also a going in to wonder. A sight-seeing tour of the self.

When I see a sheep tract across a bog I follow it. Each path has something to show me if I'm alert enough to see it.

All my pathways lead to Errigal. My heartland.

ERRIGAL: FOR MY FATHER

In your last few years
as your body hunched and greyed with age
Errigal took possession of you.

It spread its angular limbs
tightly around you, shouldering you
every so often high up towards the sky.

It filled your eyes, your imagination
with its muscular, grey bareness.
Your mind was immured in its peak.

A heathery beard clung to the slopes
of your face, a scraw on your eyes, hoary lichen
from the back of your head to your forehead.

In the evenings, at sunset, the light
lay placidly on you, coaxing a gleam
from your quartz cheek, your granite forehead.

Your language grew sharp, became spiked;
a rockfall of scree slid every day
from the steep incline of your tongue.

Slowly but surely, you were crystallised
by its citadel, its gloomy face, its spellbound wall.
It enthralled you towards its eternity.

Now when I look at the mountain
your stare is constant from every overhang and hollow.
You have taken possession of Errigal.

Translated by Paddy Bushe

AN tEARAGAIL : DO M'ATHAIR

Agus tú sna blianta deireanacha
cromadh agus liathadh na haoise ag teacht ar do chorp,
ghlac an tEaragail seilbh ort.

Spréigh sé a ghéaga beannacha
thart ort go teann. Ar ard a dhroma, thógadh sé
leis chun na spéire thú, uair sa ré.

Líon sé do shúile, do shamhlaíocht,
lena liathacht, lena láidreacht, lena loinne.
D'fhág sé d'inchinn i nglas binne.

D'fhás feasóg fraoigh ar leargacha
do leicinn, scraith ar do shúile, crotal liathbhán
ar bhínn do chinn ó bhun go héadan.

Tráthnónta agus an ghrian ag gabháil faoi
luíodh an solas ort go sochmaidh, ag baint gealáin
as grianchloch do ghruaidhe, as eibhear d'éadain.

D'éirigh do bhriathra géar agus spíceach;
clocha sciligh a sciorr anuas achan lá le fánaidh
ó mhalaidh chrochta do theangaidh.

Diaidh ar ndiaidh, chrioslaigh sé thú
lena dhúnáras rúnda, lena dhúchas dúr,
lena mhúr draíochta.
D'ordaigh sé leis thú chun na síoraíochta.

Nuair a amharcaim ar an tsliabh anois
stánann tusa orm go síoraí ó gach starrán, ó gach ball.
Tá seilbh glactha agat ar an Earagail.

ERRIGAL:
PASSAGES OF LIGHT

As a child I dreamed it, that heady road that led to all that I desired, that bright, beguiling road with an upthrust of mountains on each side, more beautiful than any mountain lauded in song or story; a road sweetened by a breath of air as fresh as spring-water, as full-bodied as the rarest wine; a road that lingers over old, fabled bridges and passes through sun-dappled villages of dawn and dusk; a road full of peaceful nooks where in ease I sit listening to the Earth sing its song of green, while below a far-off headland gushes forth in a spume of white.

From Mo Bhealach Féin
by Seosamh Mac Grianna,
a version by Cathal Ó Searcaigh.

— 1 —

On my walks around Errigal I open up and enjoy the spirited communion of being a participant in a vibrant world of grassy banks and vivid heather; of gleaming rocks and flashing bogholes.

I'm ceaselessly surprised by the wild diversity flourishing around me; the dwarf willows, the bog myrtle, the saxifrages, the small gentians, the sphagnum moss, the lush grasses.

And I'm constantly being lifted, emotionally and imaginatively, beyond my own enclosed life into the life of all, into immense existence.

And in these exquisite moments of realisation, I know that Errigal is also a part of my nature; the part, that in some measure, emboldens my imagination.

On this meditational pathway I'm compelled to bring into focus my own spiritual beliefs.

Today my religion is a creed of amplitude; an open heart that asks the branching tree and the tunnelling earthworm for the truth.

This clear mountain stream – steadfast, giving, spirited – tells me all I need to know about the Dharma.

A moss-covered stone is as edifying as any sacred scripture.

In the presence of still lake-water at Loch An Ghainimh I know the revelatory power of silence.

I feel a vibrancy in every atom of my being that brings me into alignment with blazing galaxies and with blades of grass.

After all every particle of my body comes from that primordial orgasm of matter that begot the universe. I'm an exudation of that primal energy.

Today it flows through me with an aching love to coalesce, to be whole again.

Every part of me and every part of you, every grain of sand and every blade of grass, contains a configuration of the whole.

All living matter, be it minute protozoa or a supernova, is intertwined in this bounteous weave of creation.

Seán O Ríordáin, the Irish language poet, recognised this cosmic dynamic in a poem called "Na Fan". "Níl áit ar fud na cruinne nach ann a saolaíodh sinne," is, I think, one of his most visionary insights. "There is nowhere in the Universe where we have not been born."

We live in grim times. The intricate balance in nature, that interweave of parts is coming undone.

In the name of development, economic growth and progress, we are all complicit in the ecological holocaust that is laying waste our world.

Countless species are being wiped out; radioactive waste and toxic exhausts foul our waters and spoil our air.

The detritus of prosperity, the effluent of greed, is killing the Earth.

Only when we become one ecological congregation, a wholehearted fellowship of love, swearing allegiance to the branching tree and the tunnelling earthworm, will we bring the Earth and ourselves back into a natural alignment of needs.

In these terrible times when man's inhumanity to man has grown to grotesque proportions we have to reverence ourselves.

"Reverence thyself", counselled Edward Young, author of the once esteemed but now sadly ignored "Night Thoughts".

"Reverence for life", means, according to Young, the recognition of oneself as life that wants to live among other forms of life that want to live.

In order to attain this empathy, this rapport you have to rely on your imagination – the imagination of what it is to be these other forms of life that want to live and thrive with you on the same plane of existence.

And isn't that what compassion is all about, an imaginative recognition of and a humane understanding towards all these life forms, tangible and intangible, that co-exist with us in this earthly realm.

This evening at the Dúloch in Mín an Leá I watched a Milky Way of water-lilies stretching across the stellar silence of its waters.

Further up the road where it turns off to Prochlais I marvelled at the collisions of sunset colours above Cnoc Fola, a grand wreckage of amber and violet, ivory and gold, ochre and oyster blazing across the sky.

I greeted a leafy tongue of grasses and saluted a higgledy parade of thistles by the wayside.

Here, I will attend to my own salvation, not by submitting to the words and beliefs of others but by attuning myself to the deep humming of bees in the flowering heather, to the whispering fraternity of mosses in the boglands, to the annunciations of Light on Errigal.

In Caiseal na gCorr admiring the forthright authority of a lone ash tree; the spontaneity of daisies and the patience and resolve of a bog asphodel. I feel blessed to be a part of this planetary community, this largesse of life.

I know that if I act in consonance with it, I will always have this bountiful experience.

And I will live generously.

— 3 —

I'm enjoying a quiet, outdoors Sabbath.

It's an evening of scudding clouds and murmuring water.

Out here where green life thrives I'm refreshed by birdsong and the scent of honeysuckle. I become attentive to wonders, to the white drift of daisies in a hollow, to patchy sunlight on a hill, to the chant of green foliage by the roadside.

I thank an ash tree for its nurturing breath and curtsey in front of a regal foxglove.

I'm grateful to have an intimate place in the midst of this bountiful community of green grass, birds and trees.

My senses mingle with their essences. I know that to be is a blessing. In this sacred moment I want all things to be happy.

The Earth spins, the trees sway in the wind, the light glides along a hilltop. All is alive and all is dance.

I pity those who are estranged from the Earth. There is nothing more ennobling than to touch and be touched by this beauty.

Bound here between the ether and the abyss, on the edge of edgelessness, I give thanks to this earthly fate for giving me the gift to wonder, to be surprised, to tremble.

I see the haloed head of Errigal as it gleams in a sudden burst of sunshine.

My salvation is here and not in any other world.

SANCTUARY

Here in the hollow of the mountains
it is more peaceful than a country chapel.
I walk, cap in pocket, silently
down the mossy carpet of the aisle,
down between the grass-clump pews,
and at the altar-height, stand a moment,
while a faint breeze – the altar-boy –
dispenses heather incense everywhere.

Yet in this mountain chapel there's no talk
of rule or regulation and I'm not plagued
by the brutal piety of the pulpit
threatening those who err with torment.
This is no God of Tears or God of Thorns,
God of Tyranny or God of Mercy
this God I am now looking at
but a God indifferent to my hindrance or my help.

Here it is with his life rather than his words
that whatever God there is makes himself known;
ignoring signs of reverence, veneration.
The source of all energy. Creator of the Elements.
Enough for him to stir, blossom
and push towards the light in every new-grown shoot.

His joy is the lustre of every colour,
he gives life to the air around me with his life.

With every breath I take
I breathe him from the pure air
as fresh as new-baked bread, as cool as wine.

Translated by Aodán Mac Póilín

TEARMANN

Istigh anseo in ísleán an tsléibhe
tá sé níos suaimhní ná séipéal tuaithe.
Siúlaim, bearád i bpóca, go tostach
síos cairpéad caonaigh na pasáiste,
síos idir na piúnna tortógacha,
is ag ardán na haltóra, seasaim bomaite,
is beochán beag gaoithe – an cléireach –
ag croitheadh túise fraoigh ar fud na háite.

Ach i séipéal seo an tsléibhe níl trácht
ar riail ná ar reacht is ní bhím cráite
ag cráifeacht bhorb na puilpide
ag bagairt léin ar lucht na hearráide.
Ní hé Dia na nDeor ná Dia na nDealg,
Dia na Tíorántachta ná Dia na Trócaire
an Dia seo ar a bhfuil mé anois ag faire
ach Dia ar cuma leis mo chabhair nó mo chealg.

Anseo, is lena bheatha seachas lena bhriathra
a chuireann cibé Dia atá ann é féin in iúl;
gan aird aige ar chomharthaí ómóis ach oiread
le haltú.
Foinse gach fuinnimh. Cruthaitheoir na nDúl.
Is leor leis a bheith ag borradh, ag bláthú
is ag brú chun solais i ngach brobh nuafháis.
Tá sé ag aoibhniú chugam i niamh gach datha
ag beoú an aeir faram lena bheatha.

Le gach anáil dá dtarraingím,
análaím chugam é ar an aer íon
chomh friseáilte le harán, chomh fionnuar le fíon.

— 4 —

I like to walk at night especially when the countryside is bathed in pale ivory moonlight.

I choose the bog roads mostly, rough gravelly tracts that wind their way among the hills. Errigal is always within sight, steadfast, reassuring, imperturbable. A friend.

Rarely do I meet another person on these lonesome night paths. I love this swampy solitude where the only sound is the gurgle of running water or the husky cackle of a startled moorhen or a snipe bleating like a kid goat.

Walking in the dark on this meshwork of moonlit paths I get an expansive sense of being, a sharp and intense feeling of aliveness. I seem to open up to this half-lit, nocturnal world with an acuity that I don't usually experience during the daylight.

Every sound and sight and smell comes to me with a palpable intimacy and seeps down into the soft bog of my body; the long sobs of lakewater coming ashore at Loch An Ghainimh, the massed amber light atop Achla Mór and Errigal, the delectable waft of bog myrtle in Prochlais.

The odours, gleams, murmurs of bog life fills me with a moist contentment. I become a ruminant of heather scents, shifting mists, curlew cries.

Whitman knew the empowering reach of the earthly. "Logic and sermons never convince", he declared. "The damp of the night drives deeper into the soul."

The mind is refined or indeed, as happens so often, is made coarse by how the body absorbs and then responds to the mortal and sensual experience of being in the world.

On these walks I carry a torch but I seldom use it. Even on an overcast night there is always a glimmer of light, enough to become familiar with the subtle colourings of the dark; the black gloss of peat, the grey shimmer of water, the dull bronze of heather. Colour is not absent in the bogland night. It is less substantial but more subtle in texture requiring a greater attentiveness to appreciate its muted beauty. Strangely I have better nightsight than I have day vision.

As yet the glare of artificial lights – the sodium gloaming of much of our built-up spaces – is not fouling the atmosphere here and on a bright night one can still enjoy a spectacle of stellar glory glowing across the sky.

Gazing up at a blazing night sky it is no wonder that the sheer immensity of it, its bewildering scale of time and space awakens in us a sense of awe and apprehension, a feeling of religiosity.

It is not at all odd that we have placed a ruling deity out there in that great silence, an omniscient being who governs our human affairs from afar. We feel small and insignificant when faced with this vast unknowingness. The despair of death and the fear of extinction makes us put our lives in a larger setting, hoping that our frail assemblage of blood and bone is not just happenstance.

We seek an absolute, an organising intelligence in the universe that gives us clarity, certainty and guidance.

5

An Cnoc Glas is a green, north-facing, rounded hill at the bottom of Errigal. Its cosy greenness is in sharp contrast to the stark grey eminence that looms above it. A deep hollow of crumbled rock, stunted growth and lichened boulders lies between it and the base of Errigal; a chasm of shadows to be crossed over if you intend to scale the steep north face of the mountain.

From this side, scrambling up its craggy face through trickling scree is not for the faint-hearted. It's better and safer to keep to the approved ridge-path at the back unless you are a practised climber.

Today from the top of An Cnoc Glas as the mist lifts, a veined landscape comes to light, delicate as the underside of a sycamore leaf; a gleaming wetness of ruts and cuts furrowing the terrain between townlands.

Below me a green domesticated glen flanked by tawny autumn bogs runs to the sea. Gleann an Átha.

This is my ancestral home, the hill-farmed holdings of my people.

Here I have a face, a name and a place. I belong to a sustaining communal and cultural energy. From Dún Lúiche to Gort a' Choirce.

We all have a longing to belong, a need for meaning, a yearning for love and as we age a wish for mental calmness.

Being part of this close-knit community gives me that affecting sense of well-being; a gladdening relationship with myself and a warming one with others.

This afternoon sitting on the top of An Cnoc Glas I think about those delicate channels of communion; physical, emotional, psychic that criss-cross this human landscape, connecting people and place in a subtle web of Kinship; an intricate grid of roads and paths and laylines; a social conveyance of ties and bonds and associations.

How like the human body this landscape is in its dynamic; in its complex mesh of energy.

Long before William Harvey (1578-1657), an English physician, discovered that blood circulated in the veins (and was not, as they thought at the time, absorbed as food) the ancient East knew that a network of subtle channels allowed pranic energy to flow around the body.

The meridians of Chinese acupuncture, the Chrakas of Yogic consciousness, and the humour-like conduits of ayurvedic medicine attest to this deep understanding of energy circulation in the body and also a clear realisation that imbalances and blockages of this dynamic flow cause ailments of the body and illnesses of the mind.

All these ancient therapeutic systems view the body as a network of energies and the healing of it involves setting free trapped energy and letting that current of vitality restore the person to health.

Those ancient holistic approaches make complete sense to me as curative recourses to a whole range of human illnesses both of the body and the mind. It's energising the body to cure itself.

Likewise the Earth is a living organism with its own subtle energy lines which protect, sustain and nourish it. Older belief systems, especially the Goddess cults, were much more attuned to this living Earth than present day orthodoxies and were heedful of its needs.

The Judeo-Christian-Islamic theologies are not noted for any specific ethics of ecology.

However the Hindu-Buddhist code of beliefs encourages a more venerable communion with the natural world, an acknowledgement of inter-dependance and a sense of the elemental being sacramental.

Ours is a very destructive mind-set, our voracious appetite for economic growth threatens survival.

The ruthless exploitation of the natural world and its resources is leading to global ecocide.

Impending doom lurks in the murky shadows of Prosperity.

We have maltreated and maimed Gaia, our Mother Earth.

We have convulsed her pranic life-lines, we have disordered her abilities to cleanse, heal and re-energise herself.

Human nature! We have to take stock of these two words, these two worlds; human and nature, and know that they are interdependent, realise that neither can thrive without being in harmony with the other.

Respect for the human, reverence for the Earth, these principles should be enshrined in all State and Church ethics.

We also need our economics to be attuned to ecology.

Here however, in Gleann An Átha, time still moves slowly, the enduring values of a seasonal, cyclic calendar gives meaning to life.

You get a sense of a community being connected to the natural world, to their traditions and to themselves.

It's a continuity that I find heartening.

As I look back at Errigal, it's sitting in a steady yogic posture in the sun, surveying our comings and goings with inscrutable calmness.

6

Teresa Kennedy lived the greater part of her life in a little republic of light called Caiseal na gCorr, a St Ives of the Bog.

For forty years she was consistently engaged in capturing the elusive spirit of Errigal in her luminous water colours.

She was marvellously adept at trapping those sudden shifts of light that occur in this hilly climate. Suddenly a hill lights up mysteriously mauve or a field glows in an amber mist or a sunset flush brightens up the face of a gruff lake.

Teresa was instinctually attuned to this vibrant light; this grainy, glimmery light that transfigures a morning or raises an evening to a divine perfection.

I love the oriental stillness of many of her paintings. They are small illuminated moments that glow with a lyrical intensity.

She was a seer of open spaces, a celebrant of the stellar light between hills. She made you alive to the awe of landscape; to the lingering touch of sunlight on the swell and curve of a cloud, to the glimmer of moonlight on bogpools.

In her art there is a lot that is totally familiar; the recognisable everyday sights that we are accustomed to see and yet under Thresa's visionary light they become the frontiers to another world, the gateway to a lost domain. Here Earth and sky touch, illuminate one another. The ordinary becomes the extraordinary because it is revealed anew.

Teresa trained her eye to look intelligently, to look intently.

She was focused. As far as art was concerned it was a question for her of seeing so much clearer than the rest of us, of doing to people and to places what the light does to them. Reveal them.

Conversing with Teresa was a real joy. She spoke with an assured calmness and always wisely. Life had taught her many things and that knowing gave her a canny ability to appraise the world sensibly and with wit. She once described the poems of an associate of hers "as feathers from a wayward angel's flight". One day when I played snippets of oriental music for her she remarked that they were "fragile and delicate like hankies blowing on a washing line". Grieving over a tormented friend who had a severe mental collapse she concluded, "secrets can really make you sick."

Being of upper crust English stock it was natural that she would have the formal reserve of her class. But it was never snobbish or severe. Demure, perhaps, and private, but never aloof. I loved her regal bearing, her well-bred poise and her lovely refined manners. Teresa managed to be both prudent and passionate. Getting these two polarities of affirming and suppressing in proper equilibrium is a real test of character.

Like Errigal, Teresa managed it with grace and elegance.

7

Burying Embroidery is a fascinating book by Ian Gordan, a landscape painter who lives in Mín Na nGall, a townland in the Dún Luiche area.

He also makes art works, small embroidered tapestries and buries them in landscape settings, mostly in the wild.

These offerings to the Earth are Ian's idea of integrating art into the environment. It usually is a private interment and only the artist knows the location.

Hiding something in the landscape is, I suppose, a way of creating a special relationship with a particular spot. An affinity, an intimacy is established with that place, a magical connection. Knowing something about the place that is unique to the concealer has a certain amount of witching charm about it, a necromantic allure. The sympathetic magic of Art.

Some people will say that the whole idea of it is a stupid, misguided, unsociable use of Art.

I see it more as a contemplative exercise; a pensive, ritual journey into the unknown where the artist remains attentive to each detail of his passage.

It becomes a story of taking an idea on a spirited journey.

That seems to me to be an appealing pursuit.

I guess in Ian Gordan's case that it is his homage to the Land Art movement of the seventies; a radical reaction to the capitalistic art-market.

I'm reading this book sitting on a grey, solitary boulder; an erratic, I suppose, shed by the glacial drift and looking down towards Loch Altan, Errigal is at my back.

The rending snout of receding glaciers gouged out this terrain of lakes and glens, recesses and depressions.

This furrowed upland is a sheep pasturage in the summer months. In harsh weather it is often stony and harrowed-looking but today it is radiant in its purpling swatches of heather.

A carousel of skylarks and meadow pipits enliven the air.

The bog cotton like little wooly swans sway on a floating breeze. Below me the cascading chant of Abhainn Mhín An Mhadaidh.

Now in a burst of sunshine after a light shower a Persian carpet of heathers, mosses, sedges, rushes and lichens rolls out its range of gleaming colours: lavender, ginger, burgundy, gentian, mustard, emerald, pink, pewter, puce.

And below me Loch Altan is an oval of Lapis Lazuli ringed by a gold band of sand. And behind me, Errigal gleams with a silver grey brilliance.

And like all bogs this one also hoards its buried past. Pine stumps protrude here and there like charred bones.

A Neolithic past survives in this wet, acidic preservative.

Occasionally when I'm sloshing through these ancient bogs I hear megalithic rumblings from a far distant past. Eerie it may be but I also find it reassuring, a vocal link with ancestery. Perhaps it's nothing more than a fervent genealogical imagination.

Of course we all carry a racial past encoded in our DNA and passed down from generation to generation.

Tramping these bogs and seeing ancient tree stumps, I'm mentally carried back thousands of years to a twilit prehistory.

I become very conscious that I am treading a hallowed biodiverse archive that holds a living, breathing record of its organic past.

It is a quaking womb of History.

In a moment of gratitude and in homage to Ian Gordan, an artist of this landscape, I bury his lovely book in a little grassy nook close to the lake.

And looking around at the enduring magnificence of Achla Mór and Errigal, I give thanks for my own brief human tenure on this precious Earth.

8

Drawing water from the well I watch the sun creep across the hills.

Being of these hills I want nothing more than to hold this landscape in my arms, stroke its ruddy cheeks of heather, smell the gorse in its hair, kiss its evening eyes. I like to think of myself as a citizen of the green constituency of the wild.

Whatever about the ruling government in Dublin I have my very own thrilling assembly in the garden, my Dáil of warblers, my Senate of grasshoppers whose governance is clear and lucid; a green supremacy of song.

Marcus Thrush Aurelius, my emperor of dawn and dusk, holds sway on the hedgerow, delighting me with his well-tuned truths.

Here everything is ratified by song.

Now, earth and sky merge and blend. Errigal on a lotus throne of mist graces the evening.

A millennium ago a Chinese poet remarked "a thousand years may be beyond me but I can turn this moment into an eternity."

I am a devotee of Li Po and Tu Fu, two poets of the T'ang dynasty. I love the clear-sighted clarity of their poems.

They remind me of light through doors, the light thrown out of houses on winter evenings at dusk when the doors are slightly ajar.

The wealth of that light, especially in the hilly townlands where I live, where the houses are few and far between has always been inviting.

The spill of light from these ancient Chinese poems is what draws me in.

They were also mountain parts and as devoted to their native peaks as I am to Errigal.

SPEAKING TO LI BAI
(For Stephen Rea)

I'm of that age now,
those declining years,
that I can converse
with you, precious one,
across the abyss of the centuries.

I'm sipping wine, sitting
out under the stars
on a crisp, early autumn night –
your book spread before me.
In vino veritas, you observe,

as I take joy in the juice of the golden
yellow apple of the moon
that is filling towards ripeness
over there on the summit of Errigal.
Wine ferments its own verse,

as you yourself know, dear heart,
who gave yourself to drinking and music.
The divine dissipation of Art!
And so you freed your mind
from the world's fetters and fastenings.

I think the world of you,
you most convivial of *viveurs*,
vagrant versifier, oracle of opposition,
who burst through custom, whose only loyalty
was to the business of poetry.

I want to assert
our pulse in common
when both of us celebrate
this world that does not abide.
Here's a world of trouble! A world of dreams!

You lived in interesting times,
ethnic wars, border wars,
conflict and destruction throughout the Kingdom.
You placed your trust in poetry,
as I do, for your salvation.

And you wandered through your world
travelling with restless clouds
over mountains and rivers,
sending joyful screeches to the wild geese
and having lunatic conversations with the moon.

Tonight, airy with wine,

I hear the Yellow River of poetry

flowing between the banks of the page.

There you go in the moonlight.

With my poem, I send you salutations

across the abyss.

Translated by Paddy Bushe

LABHRAIM LE LI BAI
(Do Stephen Rea)

Tá mé san aois sin anois,
ré na seanaoise,
go dtig liom mo chomhrá
a dhéanamh leatsa, a mhian,
thar dhuibheagán na gcianta.

Mé i mo shuí ag ól fíona
amuigh faoin spéir
oíche shoiléir i dtús an fhómhair
do leabhar os mo chomhair.
Tá fios i bhfíon, a deir tú,

agus mé ag baint sú as úll
órbhuí na gealaí
atá ag teacht i gcraobh
ansiúd ar bharr an Earagail.
Cruthaíonn fíon a fhilíocht féin,

mar is eol duitse, a chroí,
a d'imigh le hól is le ceol.
Drabhlás diaga na hÉigse!
Ar an tslí sin scaoil tú saor d'aigne
ó ghlais is ó gheimhle an tsaoil.

Sílim a mhór duit,
a fhir lán de mheidhir,
a fhánaí na ndán, a fháidh an dúshláin,
a bhris gach gnás is nár fhan dílis
ach amháin do chúram an dáin.

Ba mhaith liom a mhaíomh
go bhfuil cuisle ghaoil againn
le chéile agus muid beirt ag ceiliúradh
an tsaoil seo nach bhfuil seasamh ann.
Saol na trioblóide! Saol na brionglóide!

Bhí tú beo i dtréimhse dhoiligh,
dreamanna ag troid fá chríocha,
cogadh agus creach ar fud na Ríochta.
Chuir tusa do dhóchas i ndánta,
mo dhálta féin, le tú a thabhairt slán.

Is chuaigh tú le fán an tsaoil,
ag triall le scamaill shiúlacha
thar shléibhte is thar aibhneacha,
ag ligean liúnna áthais leis na géanna fiáine
is ag comhrá go gáifeach leis an ghealach.

Anocht is mé bogtha le fíon
cluinim Abhainn Bhuí na filíochta
ag sní idir dhá bhruach an leathanaigh.
Siúd tú faoi sholas na gealaí.
Le mo dhán, beannaím duit

thar an duibheagán.

9

I like to walk the russet brown uplands under the benign horse face of Achla Mór. I'm drawn to this remote area, to the deserted townlands of its foothills, to Mín na gCopóg, to Prochlais, to Mín na bPoll.

I'm moved by their green untended pastures fringed by the browns and purples of the bog; their crumbling houses draped in brambles; their small gardens buried in scrub willows; the passage of evening light across their abandoned fields and thistle meadows.

The loneliness and the hopelessness of these wiped-out townlands touch me. What were once busy settlements are now devoid of people. At nightfall where lights once beckoned from hillside houses there is only the gloom of dark.

In the sense that it lacks the living it is a landscape of absence and yet it is not without its presences. A residue of past lives still resides in the rushy fields and the empty houses.

Here, I'm drawn back to roots and sources; to gaping windows and stony hearths; to distant forebears; to ties of kin; to shared experiences. Here, I want to break the ground of forgetfulness, chop up the rooty soil of memory, reclaim bygone lives. Here I am haunted by my people's past, by what is hoarded in the layered earth of their labours.

Sometimes it seems to me that their stories, the spirit of their lives, the lore of what is lost fills the air like a pulse, like a heartbeat.

Suddenly something out of the past stirs, shows signs of life, becomes palpable. It may only be specklings of sunshine moving across lost meadows or dappled light along grassy lanes but it's enough to quicken the imagination, to rouse it into utterance.

In that fanciful state I hear snatches of talk at the corner of a field, a man levering stones out of gravelly ground, a child at play, a woman haranguing a dog in the distance. All, it seems, the earth-rooted leavings of past lives.

Subtle, faint, shadowy they arise, the transfigured forebears of these townlands. In Mín na gCopóg, in Prochlais, in Mín na bPoll they still haunt their old familiar holdings. A mere illusion, you say, but I like to believe that a timeless commonwealth of ancestral memories live on and endure, a subtle configuration of consciousness that coexists with us on a parallel plane. And sometimes by pure chance we broach these realms, these domains of future past and like Kavanagh we know that we have walked through fields that were part of no earthly estate.

This hillside neighbourhood where I live is full of the carcasses of old abandoned houses left to Time's slow mouldering ruin. Nobody here wants to obliterate a site still occupied by the spirit of the forefathers. These houses may be crumbling ruins but people sense the ancestral presences still hovering around the empty hearths. They firmly believe that it would bring bad luck to knock them down deliberately.

The tribal taboos, particularly in rural Ireland, helped to conserve a considerable amount of our ancient past; raths, fairy rings, megalithic sites, wells. These repositories of prehistory survived because of a sense of ancestral reverence coupled with a fear of the consequences if one violated a venerable site. I accept that attitudes are changing now and people generally are no longer constrained by these notions of ancestral worship. But here where I live the native community still honours these old beliefs.

So many derelict houses draped in wild ivy; so many ruins strangled by scrub hazels; so many meadows abandoned to heather; so many fields where potatoes and corn were grown, now taken over by tenacious crops of rushes and brambles. The seasonal calendar of farm routines is no longer a concern in these wiped-out communities. The reality now is that the cartwheel and the plough, the harrow and the sickle are installed in front of hillside holiday-homes to create a rural ambience.

Here, under Errigal, I walk the hills, particularly at twilight, "idir an dá sholas", as we say, a time when the snipe bleats in the darkening air and the grouse with its husky cackle flits across the wild bogs. This is also a walking meditation, a time of reflexion, a tracing of past lives, and a longing to belong to what is gone; a yearning to bring the past into the present so that it will have a future. On these walks I delve into the living sod of my memory and feel, sometimes, as if in a vision the lives of my forebears are taking shape in front of me, unearthing themselves, perhaps, out of the depths of my own racial memory.

The "Deserted Villages" is a poem in which I attempt to bring this notion to light.

— 10 —

THE DESERTED VILLAGES

At evening, in the half-light,
I see them taking shape
out of the mist that veils the dead.

My grandfather, my people's
people, I see them
working out in the open,

the men reaping in fields
that aren't there anymore,
the women milking cows

in a sunny cattle-fold,
the children playing hide-and-seek
among stooks and sheaves.

As far as my eyes can see,
the dead, teeming with life,
are gathering on the old sod,

in the small deserted villages
of the foothills, in Mín na bPoll,
in Prochlais, in Mín na gCapóg.

From the Mín of my vision
they come, those buried generations
walking steadily along.

Looking as though they miss
their old haunts, these villages
where they spent their days.

Now wending their way
homewards, their footsteps as quiet
as the night closing in.

Bound to what is unspoken,
they carry a grave wisdom, silently,
between the living and the dead.

2

In the field of the old house
this harvest evening, the fallow
ridges are shrouded in sedge.

I am heartsick for that world
that I am bound to by generations,
and that is now under scrawny grass and scrub.

I who didn't follow my people's tracks;
those who sowed and reaped, earthy people,
who lived by the customs of the place

from generation to generation, the hardy men,
who sowed their seed in womb
and in field; the sturdy women

who stood by them and worked
their hands to the bone.
I cannot follow their way,

I, who did not build a wall, nor plough a field,
who did not beget a son or a daughter of our kind,
of our kindred. A poor show

to leave them heirless now,
while their land turns barren in Mín na bPoll,
in Prochlais and in Mín na gCapóg.

3

They are immured in silence now,
the toilers, the hummock breakers
of Mín na bPoll, of Prochlais, of Mín na gCapóg.

Wordless now the once mighty Sweeneys;
the Harkins, noted for their lore;
and the O Boyles, beloved for their beauty.

There's a keening moan on the wind
that's coming west from Altan
while here a spider spins

A death shroud in the gapped
window of the old house
where long ago my people lived.

On Ard na mBothóg as mist
draws down its blackout blinds
on Mín na bPoll, on Prochlais.

On Mín na gCapóg, I stand alone.
Each ruin is interred in silence
and no word or rune will unlock a stone.

Translated by Cathal Ó Searcaigh

11

Coming from Mín an Leá, there's a sharp uphill turn on the road before you come to the little cluster of houses in Mín Na Craoibhe, and at this sloping bend there's a ruin by the wayside, a muted huddle of stones. This was once Teach Mháire Mhór, Big Mary's House. On my walk today I sit on a drystone wall close to the brambly tangle around her house. It's a day of white clouds, bright and buoyant, which lets the sun through in a lovely scattering of light. A languorous breeze shuffles about in the rushy meadow below the house and a faint rushing of water comes to me from the stream that, lower down the glen, widens out to become the Gleann An Átha river.

Errigal, a grey resplendent spire, rises in front of me. With its churchly demeanour I would not be surprised if today it summoned me with bells.

Since my youth I have been fascinated by this house, now sadly, a crumbling ruin. The reason for this intriguing hold that it has over me happens because a writer lived here in the late 1930s and wrote a book about his time in Mín na Craoibhe. That was enough for me in my younger days to think of it as a place of literary fame, a fabled spot. It was exhilarating for me to think that a real author had lived so close to my home. I also wanted to write, to see my name in print, to fraternise

with like-minded people. But in that hill-farming community where I was reared, books were a rarity. In a
world where ekeing out a living was undeniably hard,
there was little regard for the niceties of literature
and nobody, that I knew, pursued a career in writing.

My father, though, unlike the other hill farmers,
had a real fondness for books and read for pleasure. He
himself was under the spell of words and delighted in
the sound and sense of poetry.

Our house may have been poor but it was enriched
by books. My father, I have no doubt, nourished in me a
love of books, and a belief that someday I could write
one myself. In the circumstances of that place, and at
that time, my father's encouragement was courageous
and heartening.

It was my father who told me about Sean Dor-
man, the writer who lived here in Teach Mháire Mhór.
Mr Dorman was a Dubliner and a nephew of Lennox
Robinson, the well-known Abbey Theatre Playwright.

He found Mín na Craoibhe at that time, I think, an
agreeable place to live in, free and far from the mad-
dening world of belligerent nations and war-touting
politicians. Teach Mháire Mhór was vacant and available
and he took a three-year lease of it.

Here he wrote and compiled the lovely sketches
that became the *Valley of Graneen*, a memoir of his
years in Mín na Craoibhe, published in 1944, by Peter

Davies, a London publisher and with charming pen and ink illustrations by Elizabeth Rivers, a renowned artist of that time.

I was touched by the book, its honesty and its accuracy; how he evoked a place and its people in quick, keen sketches; recording a grim way of life, a stubborn subsistence living on the harsh peaty farms of Mín na Craoibhe.

It's a closely-observed account in which the author catches in detail their struggles, their modest successes and their matter-of-fact forbearance.

Encircled by treeless hills and inhospitable bogs, with no amenities, and reached only by a rutted gravel track, Mín na Craoibhe at that time was a poor isolated place, and not at all a marketable destination for a refined city-bred "fear uasal". But Sean Dorman took to it with a ready willingness and in doing so found a kind, affable, neighbourly community who welcomed him warmly.

The book is a sensitive portrait of a people holding on tenaciously and surviving on their scanty acreage of poor hilly land. Occasionally there's a tendency in the author to have uppish airs about the coarse living and the crude houses in Mín na Craoibhe but on the whole he writes about their hardships with a rare and a caring awareness.

The *Valley of Graneen* is a book that I cherish.

Rachel Giese-Brown, the great American photographer who stayed in Mín an Leá for a time in the early 1980s and documented the area and its people in stunning duotone photographs, was also drawn to Teach Mháire Mhór.

She took a photograph of what remained standing of it at that time, a stony gable-end with a gaping window and a wind-swept tree beside it. This photo is included in her magnificent book, *The Donegal Pictures*, published by Wake Forest Press in 1987.

This image of Teach Mháire Mhór may only have been a sighting and a click at the time, a snapshot commentary. But now we see that it's much more than that. It's a compelling visual narrative of a place, a people and their past. In it we see a simple and yet a complex story of human endeavours framed against the inexorable sweep of Time.

The palpable stir of history as it shapes the past, stamps the present and presages the future is evident in her photographs. Rachel in her search for evocative and significant images knows full well that everyday, history takes place even when nothing happens.

A photograph may only take a split second of execution but it represents, as Susan Sontag said, "a lifetime of preparation". A lifetime of walking around with one's eyes open. On many wonderful walkabouts with Rachel while she was taking photographs of the area, I noticed how intense her focus was; how alert she was to the unexpected image, to subtleties of light, to strong tonal contrasts and to shades of meaning. For me it was a useful lesson in intelligent looking and seeing things with a fresh vision.

Her book, *The Donegal Pictures*, is a memorable homage to this place and its people. And in these pictures Errigal is everywhere. In snow, in rain, in mist and in sun she catches and celebrates its pervasive power and its presence.

My own contribution to the memory of Teach Mháire Mhór is a poem called, "Fothrach Tí i Mín na Craoibhe"/"Ruin of House in Mín na Craoibhe" which has been a prescribed school text for senior-level Irish.

Later, walking through Mín na Craoibhe on my way to Dún Lúiche, it occurred to me how, in the four-score years since Sean Dorman was here, a pleasing change had taken place, a turn for the better; unforeseen, I'm sure, in Mr Dorman's time.

Mín na Craoibhe is no longer a poor, primitive outback. Without being showy, vulgar or unrestrained in its progress, it's now a neat settlement of snug, well-appointed homes; a lived-in place with a homely face and still holding on to its native language and its rural identity.

Today a leafy growth of trees shaded the old Cannon-family homestead. A little stream gurgled pleasurably beside it; a child in a canopied buggy slept out in the open; a farmer with a sleek, black collie-dog was trying to goad and guide a drift of noisy ewes into a sheep-pen. Life, I'm glad to say, goes on in Mín na Craoibhe with a quiet, engaged assurance.

And behind it, Errigal rises out of its bulwark of hills and ridges, showing us its ageless face of fortitude. And, although it has always loomed in the foreground of my life, I have never become indifferent to it, nor, as yet, accustomed to its enduring power.

And for me it always quickens the heavy heart and moves the dull mind.

RUIN OF HOUSE IN MÍN NA CRAOIBHE

The old house, with skeletal grace,
is making music of the wind.
Without door or window
or the shelter of slates,
every wound is a tin-whistle
making wild music.

From gable to gable
the exhausted house rises
into a storm-melody.
Such music, old house!
The likes of your lilting
has never been heard
on any windy day
in a comfortable, domestic place.

Translated by Thomas Mc Carthy

FOTHRACH TÍ I MÍN NA CRAOIBHE

Tá creatlach an tseantí
ag baint ceoil as an ghaoth;
gan doras gan fuinneog gan sclátaí dín
gach foscailt ina feadóg fhiáin
ag gabháil fhoinn.

Ó bhinn go binn
tá an teach tréighe éirithe
ina shiansa stoirmspreagtha.
Mo cheol thú, a sheantí;
a leithéid de phortaíocht
ní chluinfí choíche
ó theach téagartha teaghlaigh
lá gaoithe.

12

Ian Joyce is my neighbour in Mín an Leá and an artist of international standing. From his kitchen window he has an unhindered view of Errigal. Across the wild bogs from his house this colossal of nature stands "like a monumental installation", as he likes to quip himself. He keeps a constant eye on its changing nature; its sunny humours and its rainy sulks, its brooding winters and its brightening springs.

His keen observations are then transmuted into beautiful shapes and colours. In these images Errigal is being discovered anew each time. That's the alchemy of his art.

Ian Joyce is an Errigal man whose imagination is an open vista of wonder.

His landscapes take exciting risks, a silent daring to summon up and reveal the mystic reality of the familiar. This is not a banal venture into Blakean transcendentalism. In his landscapes Ian Joyce commutes with the commonplace in a way that is neither trite nor predictable. He is a visionary of the real, a seer who liaises with what is marvellous in the ordinary.

Whether it is a picture of an angel marooned on a wild twilit moor, a bog ablaze with autumn or a moon delicate as a seedling in an April sky, the ethereal is always conveyed with a close, earthy actuality.

A recent painting of Ian's hangs in my house. The luxuriant yellow of a sunny evening in Fána Bhuí fills my room with an other-worldly brilliance. It shines with light, the kind of lustre that surrounds old saints and mystics, the glow of icons.

Like Wendell Berry, a sublime poet of the great American outdoors who buries his cast-aside winter writings in the earth come springtime so that the old commingles with the new and the past submits to the future, Ian Joyce uses his rejected jottings and his abandoned diaries as calligraphic components in his art, thus fusing the past with the future.

Using a light solvent and brushing it across page after page of the written minutiae of his life, his personal archive is washed out and defaced. However, it is a transformative act where the text is given an afterlife; a slow release of something other than its original intention. A veiled life of rare visual patterns is elicited from the ruins and residues of the faded pages, graphic fragments that transmit past truths, perhaps, or future presentiments.

It is also, I think, an attempt to free language from its weighty load of linguistic sense and give it a new visual coherence. This approach gives his art the appearance of archaic tablets, ancient fragments of a language aglow with the lore of fresh beginnings.

Whatever linguistic traces remain are transmuted into graphic runes. A *rúnscríbhinn* beautiful as the hieroglyphics of winter ice on bog holes. It is the inscrutable speech of things; the hoarse cry of the wind across March hills; the moist, salty tongue of dripping rain; the cosmic pulse of stones.

It is also a speechlessness in the face of suffering. In a number of his large-scale installations Ian Joyce identifies with those who suffer under oppressive regimes. His homage to Jan Palach, a young Czech student who set himself alight in public as a protest against the Soviet occupation of his country in 1968 – an act of self-immolation that stunned the world – shows exactly where the artist's sympathies lie. This major installation is a suspended sculptural print that uses written material from Ian's own personal history but he violates the text as an act of self-effacement. Although an anonymity is given to the text this only amplifies its truth. Encrypted within these defaced pages is the artist's outrage against any authoritarianism. It is a work of bearing witness. By mourning Jan Palach he is also lamenting the voiceless dead of all despotic regimes. This is not an indulgent art that is created for a purely aesthetic end and Ian Joyce is not a self-righteous spokesperson for suffering humanity. He knows full well that either a lofty aesthetic or a moralising simplicity can give offence to suffering.

He also knows that art should not be used to lull us into a state of self-contended pity. Although art cannot alleviate suffering it can draw attention to it, create a compassionate awareness around it and thereby become a vehicle of socio-political change.

In his *Archive for Jan Palach* and more recently in his *Shroud for Mohammed Bouazizi*, the young Tunisian who set the Arab world ablaze after making an inferno of himself, Ian Joyce reaches out imaginatively to those afflicted by tyranny and heavy-handed ideologies. In his art he is firmly on the side of singularity, and free-thinking individualism, values that are anathema to repressive regimes.

Artworks that bear witness to the tragic destinies of our times are being made under the shadow of Errigal. Out of the nightmare of history, Ian Joyce's work casts light on the human condition, illuminating it with compassion.

13

Today I'm in Gleann Neimhe or Cró Neimhe as the elders of my childhood called it, alluding, I suppose, to the needle-like aperture at the far-end of the glen. Sitting on a rock, midway up the glen, Errigal rises in front of me, a humped bulk of grey, its top lost in a drift of cloud. A hazy sky with intense patches of blue, ceilings the glen. A cleansing breeze, up from Gleann Tornáin, refreshes me after a sweaty walk. Elsewhere I get the heady whiff of fragrant heather, out now in the purple glow of early autumn. A benediction of skylarks graces the air and raises my spirits.

They call this the Poison Glen but today its more the Glen of Paradise.

Some people come away from this place feeling that they had crossed into a strange otherworldly domain where the real and the astral converged. It's a credible feeling and a genuine reaction to this eerier enclosure of rock and bog.

Earlier, at the entrance to the glen, I met a young couple on a festive outing with their precocious eight-years-old son Jason, who was celebrating his birthday. He was a devotee of dinosaurs and an outspoken intimate of all kinds of fiendish giants, lazy ogres and foul mutants. His effusive and easy familiarity with this strange world of spooky beasts and reptilian wonders was a joy to hear.

He told me that the glen was "a magical monster-land" and that the biggest of them was a gruesome giant called "Ingo Keho" who lived in a secret cave underneath the glen. This creature had a tongue of fire and a tail of thunder.

I was only too happy to join in and contribute to Jason's world of fancy. I told him that it was rumoured in the area that every morning at daybreak, Ingo scrubbed himself with a wet raggy cloud and then brushed his teeth with a big bushy pine tree. For a little workout before breakfast he was often seen doing a hop-skip-and-jump across Errigal. I could see that Jason was humoured by these notions. "What does he have for breakfast", he asked me, his comely little face all lit up with an amused curiosity.

I told him that the usual breakfast was a big crater of rock-and-turf high fibre muesli with a barrel or two of bog-water to wash it down. But one morning, I added, Ingo was so hungry he swallowed the whole village of Dún Lúiche in one almighty gulp. A battalion of soldiers came, rammed two big poles between his jaws and spent half a day tickling his stomach until finally he vomited the village out again.

"Everybody must have been covered in poo", Jason said with a slight grimace of distaste.

"That's what you'd think after wallowing around in his belly for hours, but do you know something, Jason,"

I confided in him; "when they came out they discovered that it wasn't poo at all. Each and every one of them was dripping in a wealth of gold-dust. That's why the people of Dún Lúiche are filthy rich."

Jason's lovely parents smiled benignly and concurred that it was a very reasonable explanation for the evident prosperity of Dún Lúiche. Jason looked a little bemused, I think. The make-believe beast that he had summoned up out of his imaginings, was not perhaps, so fanciful after all. It had become a real fire-breathing dragon!

Jason and his parents had already walked a bit of the glen, and now, they were leaving for further "monster sightings", he said, in the National Park in Gleann Bheithe.

He reminded me so much of myself as a child, a head full of wild imaginings and two doting parents who looked on with pride and wonderment at what they had begot.

I shook his hand and wished him a birthday full of fabulous encounters.

"If you meet Ingo Keho," he said as they were leaving, "tell him that Jason is coming to get him." It sounded like a threat.

Mary Murray, a friend of Seamus Heaney and the wife of Diarmaid Ó Muirí, an eminent Gaelic scholar, was reared here in a small house with its back to the shimmering waters of Loch Dhún Lúiche and its face looking towards the sometimes, darkly sombre, and at other times, divinely radiant Gleann Neimhe.

At her burial service in a lovely country church-yard in Co Wicklow, attended by many distinguished mourners, including Seamus Heaney, I read a poem in her honour and prefaced it with a few remarks in Gaelic, her mother tongue.

Tá Mary ar shlí na fírinne anois ach nach é sin an tslí a shiúil sí agus í ina beatha; slí a bhí umhal, múinte, uchtúil. Slí na fírinne! Mar dhuine, bhí sí dílis ariamh dá dúchas féin agus dá dúchas Dún Lúicheach.

Do Mhary, ba é Dún Lúiche an teallach, an tobar agus an tearmann.

Ba sa spás scóipiúil sléibhe sin a d'ap a haigne. B'ann a d'fhás sí i dtreo an tsolais. Dúirt sí féin gur láidrigh Dún Lúiche í; gur ansin a fuair sí an acmhainn is án neart leis an ailse a bhí ag siúl léithe a iompar go cróga.

Nuair a bhí sí ina girseach i nDún Lúíche bhí cleachtadh aici a bheith ag cur i gcoinne bristeacha borba gaoithe agus í ar a bealach na bhaile ón scoil; gaoth ghéar gharbhshíne na gcnoc anuas ó Shliabh Sneachta.

Tuigeadh díthe agus í ag teacht i méadaíocht i nDún Lúiche nach raibh, is nach mbeadh, an saol ariamh réidh, simplí, gan stró. Ach mar a dúirt sí liom uair amháin, d'ullmhaigh an tEaragail í le seasamh ar a cosa féin is a haghaidh a thabhairt ar an tsaol go dearfach.

Anois tá Cor Úr curtha ina cinniúint.

Tá an saol fágtha ina diaidh aici agus í imithe uainn ar bhealach na nglún, ar bhealach na rún. Tá sí imithe uainn amach bealach an tsléibhe chun na Síoraíochta, a bealach féin chun an bhaile.

Léifidh mé dán ar a dtugtar "Cor Úr" lenár gcara ionúin, Mary Murray, a thionlacan ar chúrsa buan na Cinniúna.

Seamus Heaney wrote a very fine poem called "Sruth" in memory of Mary; a poem in which he summons up the stream in Dún Lúiche that she often talked about – her shining amulet of water that she always kept around her memories of growing up between Gleann Tornáin and Gleann Neimhe.

Seamus Heaney is also gone. His passing away left a gaping absence in the cultural life of our country and a deep grieving in all of us who knew and admired him.

He had that rare Orphic gift to charm, to delight and to captivate. The lyrical afflatus of his poetry reminds us constantly that he was a wonderful charmer of words. At readings he charmed his listeners with his lovely, soothing unforgettable delivery. In company he was hugely engaging; funny, erudite, and yet down-to-earth. With Seamus there was never any displays of excess; never any fame-fuelled histrionics. He was grounded in his own solidly firm integrity.

When he smiled at you, you felt singled out as if a spotlight had been turned on you.

I always felt there was something Tibetan in how he looked; the eyes and the cheekbones so alike the Dalai Lama's.

Seamus, it seems to me, practiced his own very unique kind of Buddhism; you could call it Bellaghyism; a quiet, earthy gravity towards the living and the dead. And always keeping the "spirit level", especially when one is "wintering out" on "open ground" in times of grief and trouble.

Seamus also had that lovely chuckle and grin that we associate with the Dalai Lama; little mirthquakes that creased his face into delightful upheavals.

His humour was always well-nuanced, and telling. I remember him telling a story about the time in the early seventies when he moved to Co Wicklow. He was driving around, and as yet he was unfamiliar, with the lay of things in the county. He saw a signpost for Boolavogue, the historic site where Father Murphy, the rebel priest of the 1798 uprising, made a disastrous stand. He decided to go and see the place. Very soon Seamus realised that he was lost. The little roads of Wicklow apparently had no sense of direction. They badly needed some Counciling. Anyway, he saw an elderly man by the roadside, stops, lets down the window of his car and greets the old man. After some preliminary banter he says to the man: "I want to go to Boolavogue."

"Oh, you're miles away from that place", says the old man.

"That's where Father Murphy was", enquired Seamus.

"That's right", says the old man, "but there's a different priest there now."

The point that Seamus was making with this story is that history is always contempory in Ireland. The past is never disposed of however thickly the grass grows over it. The past is always with us in the here-and-now so that it never becomes old or out of date.

Here in Gleann Neimhe, I always get the sense that the place is a repository of the past, a registry of Time. Geological eras shaped it, mythological fancies defined it. Its craggy, rawboned, rockface often has a dark, forbidding look to it, and yet, when the sun touches it, it becomes a glen of light.

One could be persuaded that on these mystic occasions "it's a *beyul*", a hidden sanctuary that is made manifest. A Shambala arising out of an apocalyptic fissure in Time.

Today in Gleann Neimhe, I feel as if I'm experiencing an expanded present; a sweet dimension of light, peace and potency. Whatever entities roam these timeless zones – yogis, pagan spirits, saints, sages – I welcome their blessings.

Clannad, one of the most enduring of Irish super-groups, are also enthralled by this mysterious Glen. It's celebrated in their music and often used as the backdrop to their promotional material. They are a magnificent group who have managed to conserve our Gaelic song tradition and at the same time modernise it. They have revived the old songs and given them a stylish, upbeat, trendy sound. Through their vibrant music they have brought the riches of the Irish language to many parts of the world, and as a result got people tuned in and turned on to Gaelic culture.

They are not manufactured stars; the fatuous product of some promotional stunt. They are the real thing, a supergroup who have endured more than fifty years in the limelight. They are successful because they are deeply rooted in a place, in a tradition, in a family.

As I leave the glen the shape-shifting aerial effects of cloud and light create a phantasmal figure above the Derryveagh mountains. Undoubtedly it's Ingo Keho.

NEW TURN

Like silence you come from the morning mist,
musk of bog-myrtle on your heather cloak,
your limbs – bright streams lapping
joyfully around me, limbs
that welcome me with skylarks.

You see me truly
in the clearness of your big lake eyes –
Loch an Ghainimh on the right, Loch Altan on the left,
both stilly blue, full of sky,
the glow of summer on their hilly brows.

And you loosen to the mountain air
your girdle of the hazy heat of May;
you loosen it, my love, you cast it off
that I may wholly see
the beloved boundaries of your body.

From Log Dhroim na Gréine at the hollow
of your back to Alt na hUillinne's elbow bend,
from Mín na hUchta, the valley of your breast,
to the red slope of your cheeks at Malaidh Rua.
My eyes glide over the hollows and curves
of your beauty.

Every love-spot, every sun-spot I'd forgotten
in my wanderings. I know now what the City lacks
and I pray for an end to exile, for shelter
here between the bright paths of your legs;
for a new turn in the poem of my Destiny.

Translated by Cathal Ó Searcaigh

COR ÚR

Ciúnaíonn tú chugam as ceo na maidine
mus na raideoige ar d'fhallaing fraoigh,
do ghéaga ina srutháin gheala ag sní
thart orm go lúcháireach, géaga
a fháiltíonn romham le fuiseoga.

Féachann tú orm anois go glé
le lochanna móra maorga do shúl
Loch an Ghainimh ar dheis, Loch Altáin ar clé,
gach ceann acu soiléir, lán den spéir
agus snua an tsamhraidh ar a ngruanna.

Agus scaoileann tú uait le haer an tsléibhe
crios atá déanta as ceo bruithne na Bealtaine,
scaoileann tú uait é, a rún mo chléibhe,
ionas go bhfeicim anois ina n-iomláine
críocha ionúine do cholainne

ó Log Dhroim na Gréine go hAlt na hUillinne
ón Mhalaidh Rua go Mín na hUchta,
thíos agus thuas, a chorp na háilleachta,
gach cuar agus cuas, gach ball gréine,
gach ball seirce a bhí imithe i ndíchuimhne

ó bhí mé go deireanach i do chuideachta.

Tchím iad arís, a chroí, na niamhrachtaí

a dhearmadaigh mé i ndíbliú na cathrach.

Ó, ná ceadaigh domh imeacht arís ar fán:

clutharaigh anseo mé idir chabhsaí geala do chos,

deonaigh cor úr a chur i mo dhán.

14

An Dúnán lies at the foot of Errigal; the mountain, imperially male and phallic, rises majestically above it.

The Dún, an earthen structure, from which the place gets its name is now a grassy embankment by the wayside, directly opposite Annie Sharkey's small bungalow. A few rocks strewn like secret texts about the place is all that remains of this enclosure.

A world, an ancient way of life, may have vanished into the Earth but the psychic memory of it endures still, I'm sure, in the stones and the soil.

Here, I get an uncanny feeling of crossing a threshold. An "uaigneas" creeps over me, a lonesomeness as if I had broached a realm of the dead, a set-apart space of enigmas.

To the Síl Lugdach generations, alluded to by Brian Lacey, and indeed, further and further back into the mythic past, it may have been a place of worship. Situated as it is on a high prominent ridge between the male grandeur of Errigal and the female allure of Oileán Thoraí, it may well have been for Lugh devotees the centre of a fertility cult.

There is no way I can test, tick and verify such a notion. It's just a vagrant thought passing through my head, as I sit here on top of the dún, held by its strong drawing-power.

Perhaps Errigal, An Dúnán and Toraí are in an active alignment with each other, a subtle force-field known to the Ancients but lost to us. Living as we are under the mottled shade of modernity, we are not usually attuned to the delicate psychic and mystic currents that inspirit our world.

Today, as I look about, Errigal in its sublime male magnificence stands at my back, and beyond, on the far horizon, a white crested turbulence broils up the sea around Tory. I'm enjoying the deep stillness of An Dúnán until, suddenly, a stir breaks the silence. It's the loud throttle and whine of scrambling quads. A group of youths, I believe, performing their motorised rituals around Dún Lúiche.

This clachan of houses in An Dúnán, once the poor homes of my people's people are now refurbished holiday houses. There's no one about today. Every path is gated and every house is under lock and key.

I cannot say that my attachment to this lonely place is unsentimental. Here, on the contrary, I feel a deep-seated yearning for the Past, for all those who were here in my childhood; Proinsias Beag and his wife Kit, Madgie John, Proinsias Annie and Sarah, John and Annie; for all those kindly people who are now gone to their eternal rest. All of my grandfather's people who graced my childhood with their many acts of care and love.

In places like this where my people once lived, I feel a vibrant racial past stirring within me; a nostalgia for origins, I suppose. Anyway, life as Nietzsche so aptly observed is lived forwards but understood backwards. Memory, however tenuous that is, is my only way to reclaim that past.

The woman in my poem, "Bean an tSléibhe", is a pen portrait of Madgie John, one of those mountain stalwarts, an indomitable spirit who endured on her own, though good and bad, into old age.

It was in her house that I first saw the *Angelus*, a cheap print of Millet's well-known painting. I was captivated by how it caught our daily life as I knew it then. The scene, a man and a woman, standing with bowed heads in a field listening in prayer to the evening bell coming from a distant church. That was a familiar scene in my childhood.

I could relate to its realism; its forceful depiction of piety and hard toil.

Unlike the few religious pictures at home and those I saw in neighbouring houses, this one was different. The more familiar religious pictures of my childhood, usually, had idealised landscapes with the stiff, haloed figures of the Madonna and Child, and floating angels. In this Angelus, there was no attempt to idealise the landscape or the figures in it. I saw simple, dignified people and not perfect haloed beings. They were poor farmers, just like those around me, pausing in prayer when the Angelus rang across the fields from Dún Lúiche church.

In Madgie John's modest kitchen in An Dúnán I began to see that paintings could express life and humanity in a deeply satisfying way.

Like everyone else, my people in An Dúnán had their regrets, their moments of joy, their personal tradgies. But on Friday, 3 November, 1922, during the Civil War, real history impinged on their quiet, remote lives.

A flying squad of Irregulars (those who were opposed to the Treaty) were staying overnight in the houses of Frank and John Sharkey when an unexpected dawn raid by Free State troopers took them by surprise. Although moderately armed and experienced in combat, they were easily surrounded and captured without firing a shot.

The eight men who were caught were Charlie Daly (Co Kerry); Sean Larkin (Co Derry); Donal Enright (Co Kerry); Tim O Sullivan (Co Kerry); James Lane (Co Cork); James J Donahy (Co Derry); Frank Ward (Dunfanaghy, Co Donegal) and Dan Coyle, a local man from Cill Ulta, Gort A Choirce.

On the 28 January, 1923, all eight of them were tried in a military court and sentenced to death. However, the death sentence was later lifted from four of them but the remaining four, Daly, Larkin, Enright and

O Sullivan were excuted by firing squad at 8.30 AM on the morning of the 14 March, 1923, at Dromboe Castle, Co Donegal.

This heinous deed of the Civil War left my grandfather's people mourning the loss of those men that they had sheltered. However quiet and uneventful their lives were up to that time, the execution of these four men left them conscious of history and the shadows cast by history.

Civil War is evidence of the concealed Furies that lie savagely within a nation's psyche waiting to be unleashed given the chance. History has shown us, over and over again, how easily that fratricidal fury can seize a people with disastrous consequences. I hope that politics, that touchy undertaking, will not drag us, ever again, down that ruinous way.

THE ANGELUS

The sky a lovely marigold hue
this spring evening in Dunlewey

And a quiet reverence in the fields
where they toil in hope of a good yield

When an Angel crosses from the church
everywhere the seed is redeemed.

Translated by Cathal Ó Searcaigh

AN tANGELUS

An spéir ar dhath Órmhuire
tráthnóna earraigh i nDún Lúiche

Agus sollúntacht i ngach cuibhreann
a bhfuiltear i mbun dualgais ann

Nuair a bhuail aingeal ón tséipéal anall
slánaíodh an síol i ngach ball.

MOUNTAIN WOMAN

1

She was a hefty woman, big-boned and fleshy
with a toothless grin and a fondness for swearing
but she was never gruff or grumpy with us
when we called in to her on a Sunday.
And she'd always make us a drop of tea
while she effed this one and blinded that one.

2

Often she'd bitch and give off about
    "the old bugger of a gauger"
who had means tested her sorely and cut back
    her pension
because she had a cow about to calf in the byre
a couple of heifers out to grass and a clatter of sheep
and when she spoke about it she'd be fuming
"In this country if you have no teeth you get the
    hardest crusts"

3

And on those same Sundays we always gave her a hand
to muck out a week-load of dung from the byre
and when we took our time with the work
playacting about and farting behind her back
she'd say: "Ah boys, come on and put a shape
        on yerselves,
a fart isn't going to manure them fields in the spring."

4

"Have youse any Jizz in youse at all boys" she says
When we were witless to argue some point with her.
"Arrah, yer all as stupid as them spring lambs
 but that's what the priests and the politicians want.
Y'see when the lot of you are big enough
 they'll have no bother rounding you up like sheep."

5

Like an old tree she stood her ground firmly
growing and withering in keeping with the Seasons.
"It's not ageing I am," she'd say, "but ripening."
And like seeds, her words settled in my young mind.
And when she'd wrap her arms tight around me
I'd feel the fat – the growth rings of her body.

6

"Patience is the highest tree in Heaven,"
she said, bravely bearing up to Death,
as it hacked away at her shrunken limbs.
Now and again I have a Mass said for her in memory
of the fruits she gave me from her Tree of Knowledge
and as she'd say herself, if she were around,

"A soft word in the right ear gets heard."

Translated by Cathal Ó Searcaigh

— 15 —

Loch Altán, a glacial meltwater, lies between Achla Mór and An Bheithigh.

Walking from Mín an Leá, I take the bog road up An Droim Dubh above Loch an Ghainimh and at the foot of An Cnoc Glas, I veer down a miry sheep tract to the lake, avoiding the boggy swamp to my left.

Today, on a sun-warmed rock by the waterside I sit and enjoy the lulling sound of rippling waves coming ashore in gravelly sand. A grey heron flies over me and comes down in a slow laboured glide and lands in shallow water to my right. Motionless it stands on long yellowish legs, its dagger-like bill ready to pounce on any small fish that strays its way.

Furthur along the shoreline, in a reed bed, I hear the quacks and whistles of mallards. The plaintive peewit, pee-wit call of lapwings; a quivery high-pitched note fills the air around me.

Here, I'm surrounded by a rugged agglomeration of mountains: Errigal, Mac Uchta, An Bheithigh and Achla Mór. What a prodigious spectacle! Today they look like a drove of wild Jurassic creatures on the move.

In truth I know little about the ancient geological convulsions that cut and shaped this landscape. Nevertheless, that does not in any way undermine my appreciation of its wild beauty.

The geological impress is everywhere. If only I could read the autobiography of a rock or the memoirs of a mountain.

I have no doubt but they would give the lie to and scoff at Bishop Ussher's famous Creationist arithmetic. On a scriptural basis he scrupulously calculated and announced in 1650 that the world was brought into being at 9.30 AM on Monday, 26 October, 4004 BC.

We know well from our deepening sense of geology and palaeontology that Ussher's account of Origins is totally ludicrous, but still, to this day, it continues to be a pervasive belief among Creationists. It's obvious that fake news abounds for a long time.

I revere this world and the orgasmic shudder that created it 13.5 billion years ago.

A number of years ago, the ESB wanted to erect pylons across this landscape under Errigal. But led by Dee Brennan, the community bonded together to become an urgent and a weighty voice of protest. This collective stridency made good. The ESB scrapped their misguided plans to the relief of all of us who opposed them. It would have been an act of desecration to foul up this lovely landscape with unsightly pylons. I have seen them elsewhere, in Wales especially, striding monster-like across the Snowdonia countryside, their looks grim and ominous; their strut and swagger menacing.

I shuddered at the thought of having these forbidding presences appear in this landscape.

In a place that instils a sense of well-being in oneself and a feeling of awe at the magnitude and grandeur of the Creation, it would be utterly disquieting to have these obtrusive pylons shatter that serenity. As well as that they would destroy the unaffected naturalness of the place. We need to augment places like this, not despoil them.

I walk along the shore to the catchy strains of sloshing water and weave my way in and out of small sandy alcoves and through a parquetry of autumnal heather. Then I clamber over a ridge of grey lichened boulders at the Beithigh end of the lake until I reach Altan farm.

This place never fails to please me.

"Romantic" is a word often used to describe the allure of Altan. Although hackneyed, the word has merits as a tribute to this endearing place. Its secluded charm, its small crenelated castle-like ruin by the lakeside and its natural amphitheatre grandeur creates that grand romantic notion of enchantment.

What is now this intriguing ruin by the waterside was built as a summer residence, it seems, for John Oban Woodhouse, a Dublin-based solicitor who purchased 1,500 acres of rough mountain grazing around Loch Altan in 1844. What we see today is a sizeable enlargement of a house that was already there before Woodhouse bought the property. It belonged probably to the Sweeney Clan who farmed here in Altan and Mín na gCapóg and further along the lake in Prochlais. Woodhouse constructed his own way-in to the farm; a rough, stony avenue that branches off the main Errigal road just before Loch An Ghainimh. In its day it facilitated a horse and carriage to drive into Altan. Now it's a much-used path for hikers and hillwalkers to access this beauty-spot.

In 1848, Mr Woodhouse leased the grazing rights to Altan to a Scotsman; a Mr Wright who flocked the mountain with a 1,000 strong herd of the Linton breed of black-faced Scottish sheep. This incensed the local sheepmen whose mountain pastures were drastically reduced by this take-over. The "caoirigh brocacha" were not at all a welcomed breed to the mountain.

It was the beginning of the Sheep Wars of the 1850s, the land agitations and the struggle against cruel, overprivileged landlords in our area. With the scrape and grind of their desperate lives, the locals stood in sharp contrast to the ostentatious living of these well-off landed gentry. Their hardships and the grievous injustices of the system led the local population into covert reprisals.

In December, 1856, the resident Altan farm shepherd, Mr James Lillico from the Western Isles of

Scotland, was attacked at night, robbed and the house ransacked by a group of Molly Maguires. Three score sheep were also stolen off the mountain that night. Mr Lillico himself was severely threatened and warned to get out and return back to his country.

It was the beginning of the Sheep Wars in Donegal; an intense campaign of retribution levelled, mostly, at the flocks of these foreign sheep-owners. The animals were either stolen or slaughtered here on the mountain.

Altan Farm as far as I can tell was worked and the house occupied by various Scottish shepherds until the late 1890s when the farm was abandoned and in the ensuing years the house fell into disrepair and gradual dereliction. Maguire and Patterson, the safety match manufactures, owned Altan Farm for a period in the 1930s and 1940s but they sold it off to a Swiss businessman who, it seems, never came next or near the place.

The house is now a skeletal ruin open to the elements, the floor sloppy with sheep droppings. It's a sizable two-storey building with four big fronting windows onto the lake, which, I imagine, let a lot of light in to the upstairs bedrooms and also to the living quarters downstairs. The remnants of a partitioning wall at ground level indicates that this area was divided in two; a roomy kitchen I assume, (the fireplace is still extant) and some kind of front room, a parlour perhaps, or a dining room.

High up, I can still detect signs of paint, a faded rose pink pastel on a cracked bedroom wall. It sets me wondering about the former occupants of the house, and their lived human lives in this remote place. We have no images of this house in its lived-in-days. What a pity! A footnote or two, a few folkloric memories, and the rest, whole lives gone unaccounted for, forgotten; their days and labours consigned to the Void.

But I'm inclined to believe that something of what they were; a thought, a deed, a rare moment of joy; something of the living pulse of their lives persists here like seed in the furrows of Time.

In abandoned places we often get this inexplicable sense of soundings as if an older generation is voicing itself through us. It's the ever-present presence of the past!

Today the house lies in splendid isolation, the mouldering ruin of a bygone age; keeping its secrets and arousing our curiosity.

Although beautifully situated on this grassy expanse by the water, the house is prone to high gusting winds blowing in off the lake. That's why they had to build a parapet of stone to protect the roof tiles from striking blasts. So far that bulwark has withstood the weathering of Time.

I sit in the sun and picnic on coffee, cheese and oatcakes. Any harshness in these craggy hills around me is now mellowed by a soft clear light. After days of rain the waterfall above the house is a spume of gushing white and the hillsides gleam green and fresh. Out in the water, as if chasing its own tail, a gentle breeze whirls about in the lake.

It's so still except for the kraa-kraa of wheeling crows. Earlier I saw a dead sheep below the house. The foul smell of rotting flesh comes to me now as these scavenging birds swoop down on the carcass and begin their mess.

I recall a painful incident from my childhood when my mother and myself came out here hoping to rescue Molly, our pet ewe, who had become trapped on a bare, rocky ledge on Beithigh. For more than a week she had been stuck on a grassless shelf and unable to climb back up to safety. Where we found her, it was too risky for either myself or my mother to attempt a rescue. That day we watched her agonising death as the hoodie crows pecked out her eyes. That disturbing incident is the subject matter of my poem "Caoineadh", translated here by Seamus Heaney.

In the early 1700s during the Penal Laws, when Catholics in Ireland were beleaguered by repressive laws and their clergy cruelly persecuted, Father Terence Craig, a local priest, went into hiding here in Altan. But he was found out, the Red Coats came, hounded him down and let their vicious dogs loose on him. There's a small memorial to him on the Achla side of the lake, not far from Altan Farm, where this ruthless murder took place.

As I leave Altan Farm and walk back along the curve of the lake, I come across another dead sheep, its flesh picked clean with nothing left but a white mesh of bones. As I was passing, a light breeze blew through it making it whistle like a reed.

To my left Errigal has a long vapoury white cloud fluttering above it. It reminds me of a "Kata"– the white silk scarf given to me often in Nepal and India and draped around my neck as a blessing.

SHEEPMAN

His stiffening hands, his knobbly bones,
carry sixty years of hardship and hardiness;
of endless grappling with the brutal tyranny
of the mountain there above Loch Altáin;
mean hungry land that for years fed off
the sweat of his labours leaving him as spent
and skeletal as a weathered old bog-stump.
And the wishes that sprouted in the field
    of his heart
withered away for the want of light
out there in the cloudy gap of Prochlais
where the sky but seldom smiles
and the sun gives only the odd wry laugh.

Stuck there under the hulking shadow of Achla Mór,
no woman has ever thrilled him with the lark-song
of her kisses nor has any jubilation of love
ever had a chance to nest in the warmth of his breast.
His flock of sheep have the run of the place
from the Mín an Mhadaidh river to the top
    of Beithigh
but he himself since youth has been penned in
and bound by the menacing ditches
of his deprivation, except nights when the
    wee drop's

gone to his head, that's when his fancies leap
the mind's ditch, becoming like winter's
    hungry sheep
foraging for grass among nooks and crannies.

There's times when death sends shivers through him
when he sees a scattering of bones on his way
or when his dogs maul a fresh carcass
out in those lonesome hills where he wanders alone.
And just as the lard and the old dripping
of his daily fry-ups upset his stomach and guts,
the darkness lies heavy on his mind, the dank
gloomy dark that swills down from Achla Mór
at nightfall and sours all his thoughts.

He is there all night in his bare-flagged kitchen
slumped in his chair before the fire
muttering loudly to himself to keep the loneliness
at bay, cursing it away if only he could,
the black terror that snarls at him from the dark
waiting to sneak in given half a chance
to gnaw at his head and plunder his mind,
just like the big grey rats that claw and tear
at the ceiling above him when he falls silent.

Years ago his heart would pound and thump
with pride when the Big Drum paraded
triumphantly on St Patrick's Day in Falcarragh.
Nights now as he lies alone in his bed he hears
the muffled drum of his own heart
as it weakens, loses its beat, begins to falter.

Translated by Cathal Ó Searcaigh

EXILE'S RETURN

He's back tonight to a deserted house.
On the doorstep, under a brilliant moon, a stark
shadow: the tree he planted years ago is an old tree.

Translated by Seamus Heaney

PILLEADH AN DEORAÍ

Teach tréigthe roimhe anocht.
Ar an tairseach, faoi lom na gealaí, nocht,
scáile an tseanchrainn a chuir sé blianta ó shin.

LAMENT

I cried on my mother's breast, cried sore
The day Mollie died, our old pet ewe
Trapped on a rockface up at Beithí.
It was sultry heat, we'd been looking for her,
Sweating and panting, driving sheep back
From the cliff-edge when we saw her attacked
On a ledge far down. Crows and more crows
Were eating at her. We heard the cries
But couldn't get near. She was ripped to death
As we suffered her terrible, wild, last breath
And my child's heart broke. I couldn't be calmed
No matter how much she'd tighten her arms
And gather me close. I just cried on
Till she hushed me at last with a piggyback
And the promise of treats of potato-cake.

To-day it's my language that's in its throes,
The poets' passion, my mothers' fathers'
Mothers' language, abandoned and trapped
On a fatal ledge that we won't attempt.
She's in agony, I can hear her heave
And gasp and struggle as they arrive,
The beaked and ravenous scavengers
Who are never far. Oh if only anger
Came howling wild out of her grief,

If only she'd bare the teeth of her love
And rout the pack. But she's giving in,
She's quivering badly, my mother's gone
And promises now won't ease the pain.

Translated by Seamus Heaney

CAOINEADH

Chaoin mé na cuileatacha ar ucht mo mháthara
An lá a bhásaigh Mollie – peata de sheanchaora
Istigh i gcreagacha crochta na Beithí.
Á cuartú a bhí muid lá marbhánta samhraidh
Is brú anála orainn beirt ag dreasú na gcaorach
Siar ó na hailltreacha nuair a tímid an marfach
Sna beanna dodhreaptha. Préacháin dhubha
    ina scaotha
Á hithe ina beatha gur imigh an dé deiridh aisti
De chnead choscrach amháin is gan ionainn iarraidh
Tharrthála a thabhairt uirthi thíos sna scealpacha.
Ní thiocfaí mé a shásamh is an tocht ag teacht tríom;
D'fháisc lena hucht mé is í ag cásamh mo chaill liom
Go dtí gur chuireas an racht adaí ó íochtar mo chroí.
D'iompair abhaile mé ansin ar a guailneacha
Ag gealladh go ndéanfadh sí ceapairí arán prátaí.

Inniu tá mo Theangaidh ag saothrú an bháis.
Ansacht na bhfilí – teangaidh ár n-aithreacha
Gafa i gcreagacha crochta na Faillí
Is gan ionainn í a tharrtháil le dásacht.
Cluinim na smeachannaí deireanacha
Is na héanacha creiche ag teacht go tapaidh,
A ngoba craosacha réidh chun feille.
Ó dá ligfeadh sí liú amháin gaile – liú catha

A chuirfeadh na creachadóirí chun reatha,

Ach seo í ag creathnú, seo í ag géilleadh;

Níl mo mháthair anseo le mé a shuaimhniú

    a thuilleadh

Is ní dhéanfaidh gealladh an phian a mhaolú.

16

Over the past century and a half we have a rich catalogue of Errigal portraits. Artists have observed the mountain in light and in shade. It has been painted in its various weathers and in its many moods. It has been depicted in grey starchy rain and in volcanic outbursts of colour; in banks of broody mist and in convulsive twitches of light; we see it in hazy blue spells and in sombre grey days. Paul Henry (1876-1958) did one of his iconic blue mountain paintings of Errigal. It also appears in the landscapes of Joseph William Carey (1859-1937); Frank Mc Kelvey (1895-1974); James Humbert Craig (1877-1944); and many other well-known painters.

I should also mention Patrick Carey's black and white Errigal film which was shot in the early 1960s. It's a spectacular evocation of the mountain charting its changes through the four seasons. It has a cinematic sweep as it circles the mountain, exploring it in light and in shade, mapping out its nooks and its crannies, sifting through its tumultuous cloud cover, revealing it in all its moods and weathers. This forceful and exacting film is a masterful portrait of Errigal and one that has informed my own vision of the mountain.

As an iconic landmark, Errigal has become the familiar visual cliché for Donegal tourism. But aside from that predictable poster image, it is also the stimulus for many gifted artists to engage with it at a more exacting level and to divine something of its primordial mystery. In their art, these painters have brought forth its raw elemental energy, and also, its boundless charisma.

In their work I detect a prescient sense of what is hidden.

In many of these paintings, Errigal is a figure more than a landscape. The craggy features, the folds and plaits, the lofty presence has the character of a courtly sitter. In these portraits there is no need to overfill the composition with extraneous details. Errigal can stand on its own. It has the power, the star magnetism to fill a canvas or a screen.

At present there are many accomplished artists and artisans working in the Errigal area. With their stir and sparkle they have helped in no small way to make this place a bohemia in the bogs.

They certainly have made life here more spirited, more exuberant. All participation in the Arts is, I believe, participation in the lives of others.

We always need the inspiration, the vision, the stimulation of the creative artist in our society to open up new outlooks for the future, to provide insightful perceptions of the present, and to suggest a reliable reading of our past. The artists, as Ezra Pound said, "are the antennae of the race".

The creative artist is always, I believe, a challenger to our conformities. They want to wake us up not put us to sleep.

The Errigal Arts Festival itself, a colourful extravaganza of cultural diversity which takes place every year over a two-three-week period in July shows the robustness of the arts scene in North Donegal. This festival is a spectacle of the familiar and the foreign and has over the years impacted the social and cultural life of Donegal with its persuasive power. Like a latter-day Johnny Appleseed the Errigal Arts Festival has scattered many summer seeds in our creative consciousness; the apple-bright seeds of ideas that have taken root in the collective imaginations of our artists. The festival has been a liberating jolt of joy to the Spirit.

We have an innovative State-funded Art Gallery in Gaoth Dobhair. It's situated in the Páirc Gnó complex of business enterprises. Under the discerning and encouraging curatorship of Úna Campbell it has shown the wide range and scope of the creative arts in the Gaeltacht.

Ealaín na Gaeltachta is an agency that has played a crucial role in the development, the promotion and the strengthening of the arts here in the Gaeltacht. They have a keen vision of the arts as a transformative medium within the community and they enact these policies with a refreshing lift of enthusiasm. They risk new options, they shape new strategies. They realise that art at its most acute resists outdated assertions and dulled assumptions. We are lucky to have here in the Gaeltacht an arts agency that is both practical and visionary and totally on the side of creativity. They support the *La vie de Bohéme* around Errigal.

As a writer I envy the painter.

As I speak, as I write I'm giving birth to words.

Words that are smeared with the afterbirth of ambiguity.

Words that need to be nourished in the school of meaning.

Words that eat, sleep and excrete in the house of sense.

Words that scream and smile, laugh and cry in the lap of language.

A painter's little tube of colour speaks with a clear, pristine silence.

Raw umber, sap green, yellow ochre, cadmium red, burnt sienna are heedless of vocabulary, unmoved by utterance and yet they are eloquent. They convey their meaning wordlessly.

Writers have to confront their readers with words that carry the nightmare of their histories, the trauma of their origins on their backs.

Words that are worn out by circulation, bewildered by spin, wearied by cliché.

A painting speaks volumes ... in silence.

I envy the painter's brightly minted currency of colour.

Indigo, vermillion, magenta, verdian can be worked and kneaded into an easy expression – a lucid speech untroubled by words.

Paintings elude words and yet they convey meanings.

They are eloquent by their silence.

17

I haven't that restless passion for peaks that drives
real mountaineers to undertake perilous climbs in
ferocious terrains of snow and ice, crossing yawning
crevasses and ascending frightening precipices. I can
understand their intense need to push themselves to
the limits of human endurance. I applaud their daring
nature. I'm afraid I have nothing of their dauntless
courage or their desire to conquer some hard, intrac-
table peak or other.

I have been fortunate though to be at different
times in my life up close to many of the world's great
mountain ranges: the Annapurnas and Everest in Nepal,
the Atlas mountains in Morocco, the Rockies in the
USA, the Swiss and French Alps. All bright, magnificent
kingdoms of snow, their white rampards a colossal
challenge. But those dizzy heights were not for me.
I was happy to stand and watch in prayerful wonder.

Today, though, I will climb 2,466 feet to the upper-
world of Errigal. I stated earlier that I was reluctant in
recent times to climb the mountain; that I was happy
to observe and praise it on my walkabouts around it.
But for the sake of this narrative, I feel now the need
to experience the climb again.

A friend leaves me off at the usual starting point
and I continue my climb up the steep zigzag path along

the shoulder of the mountain. The ascent is easier now since they repaired and gravelled this upward path.

Earlier there was a splash of rain and a thick wooly cloud like a tea cosy lowered itself over Errigal but now it's lifted again and the top is enticingly clear.

Halfway up I meet a tall woman striding effortlessly down the path. She stops and steadies herself between two ornate trekking poles. When she speaks I notice a plummy English accent. Her freckled outdoor face is lit up in rapturous wonderment as she tells me about her uncanny experience.

For the past five months she had been grieving the sudden death of her dear mother. She had given up an executive job in the fashion world, stopped partying and withdrew into her own nether regions. But on top of Errigal she heard her mother's voice coming to her there in a blaze of light, assuring that she had crossed over and urging her daughter to live life to the full. Regrets, her mother told her, were what mostly pained the unliving. Marcella, her daughter, was now in high spirits by this liberating announcement and was ready to embrace the world with renewed vigour. As she leaves she plants a hot kiss on my cheek and bounds off down the path singing "Morning Has Broken". I wish her many happy dawns.

Towards the top, a young man in a maroon track-suit and goggles passes me by like a scurrying breeze.

I hear snatches of rap music coming from his loosened earpiece; a thud-thud litany of expletives. It's his way, perhaps, to a peak experience. He reaches the top, does a few brisk press-ups and then heads down the mountain again.

It takes me about an hour to reach the top, a slow relaxed climb with plenty of relief stops. Nevertheless, I feel spent and my breathing is strained. But after a slight dizziness and a flurry of heartbeats, I'm sitting on the topmost point of Errigal. A little rest, a few gulps of invigorating mountain air and I regain my strength.

It's a sobering thought to think that one is sitting on a peak that is at least 500 million years old. How meagre our life-span is, our little flash of existence, compared to this wild infinitude. Thinking about that leaves me bewildered and this is no place to be thrown off balance.

Knowing full well that Errigal is indifferent to my vulnerabilities, my inconsistencies, my dutiful attempts at portraying it, and even, my being there at all, I settle myself down atop its lofty crown and enjoy an unimpeded view of North West Donegal.

In this clear sunshine everything has a purity of outline; the lovely crescent of mountains from Sliabh Sneachta to An Mhucais; the green latticework of fields; the crystal shimmer of lakes and streams, the glaze of white buildings; the ceaseless dazzle of the Atlantic.

I can see the back strand below Falcarragh and it looks like a canvas primed with light.

Indeed this late August landscape shows a strong painterly quality, an instinctive and immediate use of warm vibrant colours; a masterly touch in harmonising tone and texture with a brilliant range of greens and browns, red and russets, ambers and ochres. It's a finely structured composition worthy of admiration and even more than that it's worthy of awe.

This ample landscape of distances, solitudes and happenstances stirs up my imagination and makes me reach for words, however inadequate they may be, to characterise it, and to make sense of it. But it remains elusive, beyond the range of words. The sibilant intricacies of running water, is perhaps, what best gives voice to this primordial vastness. But alas that arcane speech has not yet been decoded.

Sitting here on my airy perch above the abyss, I note down these lines:

Of the past, of the future,
these Errigal stones
speak in sibyl tongues.

———

In their passing, winds
have written their own epitaphs
on this white rockface.

———

Lofty and lonely
Errigal carries her agelines
to the crack of doom.

I take a last look at this softlit landscape; its bald mountain-tops, its eyebright corries, its long-limbed headlands, its brood of islands, its stout settlements, all its features and expressions from mountain to sea. I leave in an attitude of gratitude. For me it's joy and it breathes pure.

Descending I step gingerly along the bare rim, avoiding as best I can, a group of jostling teenagers who are high-stepping their way to the top.

As I come down the mountain from that spirited, sky-high stillness, I feel I'm coming back into the world of the familiar again. A steady stream of traffic hums along the main road and further away I hear the snarl of a heavy vehicle as it cranks up a gear coming up the brae from Duibhlinn.

In the carpark my friend is waiting for me. As I sit into his car he grins mischievously, "You're back to Earth again are you?"

18

The old stationhouse at Caiseal na gCorr is a place dear to my heart. Once a busy station on the now defunct Loch Swilly narrow-gauge railway line, it was until recently a gaping windswept ruin alone and abandoned to the silence of the bog. Josephine Kelly, a young enterprising woman from Dún Lúiche, bought it recently and with admirable taste and determination restored it to its former style and spirit.

There's something in the energies of the place that draws me to it again and again. Something that puts me in touch with my own creative energies. The fact that it was owned at one time by distant relations of mine gives me (or so I believe) a sense of preferment there; a sense of belonging.

My great aunt, Ann Friel, who lived in Glasgow, bought it in the late 1940s when the Loch Swilly Railway Company were selling off their assets. She was hoping, I believe, that one of her Glasgow born-and-bred children would make a home in Caiseal na gCorr. That never happened. A lonely outpost in the dank brooding bogs of Donegal was not to the liking of any of them. They shunned the place. Over years of neglect the old station became a sad, forsaken ruin until Mrs Kelly took it under her painstaking care and gave it a new viable lease of life. I'm delighted by this fortuitous turn of events. A crumbling cast-aside building has been rescued and restored beautifully.

On a rise above the station where I often sit I have a clear view of this rippling landscape of hill ridges and hollows. In the background a crescent of surging peaks with Errigal topping them all, a crescendo of grey, fills the air with resounding power.

Today as I sit here, little riffs of wind blow around me and from below I hear the lilt of running waters.

From this vantage point I see scrawny bits of farmland spread out across this hilly terrain. These are the gaunt peaty fields that my forebears scraped out of the wilderness so that they could eke out a living.

In my mind I can hear the rasp and grind of their struggles as they wrestled with rock and bog and weather, taming the wild into farmsteads of tillage and pasture. Their stout-hearted toil left us this continuing legacy of green in the midst of boglands.

This is my heartland, my home, where I belong; rooted as Yeats said, "In one dear perpetual place".

This worked landscape is a book that holds the history of my people. Here something of their fears and losses, their desires and longings, their successes and sorrows are buried in this "domasach", the layered sheets of peaty soil that make up our fields and our agrarian narrative.

At Caiseal na gCorr I'm reminded of my "Dúchas". Some words defy translation and Dúchas is one of them. It's a complicated web of meanings and associations around the notion of birth right, ancestral affinity, native tongue, patrimony and heritage.

That lexical baggage is enough to overburden any word.

Personally I like to think of the Dúchas as the cultural endowment I received from my people. Here at Caiseal na gCorr I sense that it's not an inert endowment but a living source of vitality. As a poet it's my task to channel it into a new permanence.

I'm also aware that my community extends not only in place but also in time; that all those who died in these hill farming townlands are not remote figures in the dead past but a part of my own flesh and blood. A genealogical imagination, I believe, colours my outlook. That's not uncommon in the Gaelic world. It's always been a strong impulse in Irish-language poetry.

In a sense my own poetry is essentially devotional; a reverence for tongue, place and tradition. The place names of this area reverberate throughout my poems. The cultural experience and the linguistic heritage encapsulated in these names are important to me. These names are sources of historical memories, vital transmitters of the mindset of my people. When these names are anglicised they lose their original meanings, their poetry and their music. They become a soulless code, lost in translation.

Caiseal na gCorr for those who are not familiar with Irish is merely a name signifying a place but its rich inner life of lore goes unheeded.

A "Caiseal" can incorporate a whole range of diverse meanings. It can be interpreted as an ancient stone fort, a breastwork, a church boundary wall, a clamping of turf-sods, a spinning top, the castle in chess.

"Corr" is equally loaded with meanings. It can be a bird of the crane or heron kind; a long-necked person, a rounded hill, a corn of the foot, an odd person, an outsider, a queer person, a bog-hole in a hollow, the horn of an anvil, a snout, a conical hill.

You will find this and much more in Dinneen's *Irish-English Dictionary*; an extraordinary compendium of riches. I like to think of this rare wordbook as our "notes towards the definition of culture".

This detailed naming of the land that my forebears did was their way to transform the wilderness into a place where they could feel at home.

For a lot of people, nowadays, the landscape is silent. They no longer have the name to invoke the spirit of a place. You can't converse properly with a hill, a field, a hollow or a rock without addressing it by its name. That's what my grandfather, Joe Sharkey from An Dúnan, used to say.

Caiseal na gCorr station is also a great vantage point for photographers who want to get a full-blown dramatic shot of Errigal. It was a special place for Jan Voster, the great Dutch photographer, who conveys this Errigal landscape in his pictures with an exhilaratingly fresh vision.

In his *Landscape of Remembrance* series of photographs he follows the trail of the old Loch Swilly Railway line on its stubborn sweep through the rugged highlands of Northwest Donegal from Letterkenny to Burtonport, interpreting the landscape and interrogating the ruins and the remnants of this disused line.

In his *Caiseal na gCorr* book of photographs he observes closely the seasonal work schedule of local farmers. It is primarily a work of topographic photography but with a warm human dimension to it.

Jan has sadly passed away and I miss our walks and talks through fields, across bogs and up hills as he searched for the meaningful image; the one that was imbued with a pristine, clear-sighted clarity. He had a great fondness for the work of Minor White, an American photographer who affirmed many of Jan's own approaches to Art. One of White's Zen-like affirmations was Jan's own modus operandi. "Remain still until the object of your attention affirms your presence."

I often noticed that Jan looked at things as if in a trance-like state before he clicked the shot. He was creating a psychic connection, he used to say, with the object of his attention.

A film based on Jennifer Johnson's novel *The Railway Station Man* was shot at the old stationhouse in Caiseal na gCorr. In Donald Sutherland and Julie Christie it had real stardom in its cast.

The crew built a big impressive set around the original building, which, for the duration of the filming, was a great local attraction. For a short spell we were transported to Tinseltown. Julie Christie, the beautiful heroine from Doctor Zhivago, walked in our midst.

Unfortunately, and unlike, the popular success of *Ryan's Daughter* – the other great David Lean epic which has to this very day created a spin-off in tourisim for West Kerry – *The Railway Station Man* was a flop and is now largely forgotten.

I remember advising a young, giddy crew member against cutting down a particular fairy thorn-bush which he wanted urgently to embellish a corner of the set. He scoffed at my "airy-fairy superstitions" as he said, and went ahead and cut down the bush regardless of old beliefs. Much later when the filming was over and the set dismantled and taken away, I came across the dead thorn bush, ditched ignominiously by the wayside. It occurred to me at the time that it did not bode well for the film.

AT CAISEAL NA gCORR STATION

Here at Caiseal na gCorr station
I tracked my own secluded place,
my sanctuary, and my escape.
Here I am on the one note
with what's in me, what's around me.
Here I can feel my roots
as I survey the territory of my people
around the foot of Errigal
where they are three centuries settled
on the grassy hill-pastures
from Mín a' Leá to Mín na Craoibhe.
Here, spread out before me
just like an open book,
is the whole wide range
from Doire Chonaire to Prochlais.
Above me and below, I see the holdings
that were wrested from the jaws of wilderness.
This is the anthology of my people,
the manuscript they laboured over
with their sweat for ink.
Here every field is a stanza
in the great poem of cultivation.

Now I read this epic of determination
in the green vernacular of the holdings
and it is no more or no less than *pietas*
when I throw down my challenge to nothingness
as my people wrestled with their wilderness
until their grit and doggedness
earned them their due.

Here I feel poetry *can* make something happen.
I feel the stir of meaning, of my own meaning
pulsing to the heartbeat of my people.
And all of this overcomes desire, gentles thought,
dissolves the irreconcilable in the here and now.

Translated by Paddy Bushe

ANSEO AG STÁISIÚN CHAISEAL NA gCORR

Anseo ag stáisiún Chaiseal na gCorr
d'aimsigh mise m'oileán rúin
mo thearmann is mo shanctóir.
Anseo braithim i dtiúin
le mo chinniúint féin is le mo thimpeallacht.
Anseo braithim seasmhacht
is mé ag feiceáil chríocha mo chineáil
thart faoi bhun an Eargail
mar a bhfuil siad ina gcónaí go ciúin
le breis agus trí chéad bliain
ar mhínte féaraigh an tsléibhe
ó Mhín a' leá go Mín na Craoibhe.
Anseo, foscailte os mo chomhair
go díreach mar a bheadh leabhar ann
tá an taobh tíre seo anois
ó Dhoire Chonaire go Prochlais.
Thíos agus thuas tchím na gabháltais
a briseadh as béal an fhiántais.
Seo duanaire mo mhuintire;
an lámhscríbhinn a shaothraigh siad go teann
le dúch a gcuid allais.

Anseo tá achan chuibhreann mar a bheadh rann ann
i mórdhán an mhíntíreachais.
Léim anois eipic seo na díograise
i gcanúint ghlas na ngabháltas
is tuigim nach bhfuilim ach ag comhlíonadh dualgais
is mé ag tabhairt dhúshlán an fholúis
go díreach mar a thug mo dhaoine dúshlán an fhiántais
le dícheall agus le dúthracht
gur thuill siad an duais.

Anseo braithim go bhfuil éifeacht i bhfilíocht.
Braithim go bhfuil brí agus tábhacht liom mar dhuine
is mé ag feidhmiú mar chuisle de chroí mo chine
agus as an chinnteacht sin tig suaimhneas aigne.
Ceansaítear mo mhianta, séimhítear mo smaointe,
cealaítear contrárthachtaí ar an phointe.

19

Co Donegal, where I live, is geographically in the North but politically in the South. Personally I like its sort of indeterminate, borderland position. These sort of places tend to be enigmatic and ambiguous; places where different ideas, different identities, different histories meet and challenge each other. These places are frontiers. From here we can develop new approaches, explore unknown territories of the imagination. Donegal artists like Brian Friel, Frank McGuinness, Ian Joyce, Altan and Clannad have all drawn inspiration from the county's frontier-like location. It has conditioned how they have reshaped and renewed the tradition.

I myself live in an area where the interaction between Gaelic and English is most challenging. The Gaeltacht. As Gaelic speakers we are adapting and absorbing, aligning our language to the needs and nuances of our time. We listen to *sean-nós* singing on ghetto blasters made in Japan. We tell stories around our German-made radiators. You may be a highly esteemed traditional singer totally tapped into the *Dúchas* and yet live in a mock-Tudor-thatched-hacienda-style house. Our *Dúchas* gone Dada, you could say. A friend of mine has a libidinous tomcat called Pangur Bán, shaggy from too many prowling, erection-packed nights. Another friend has a little soulful-looking Mini car called An

Bonnán Buí named after Cathal Buí Mac Giolla Ghunna's famous "Yellow Bittern" poem. In my oriental draped kitchen I sometimes sing "Caoineadh na dTrí Muire" to the air of "Lady Madonna". Lovely outrageous ways of repossessing the tradition and breathing new life into it. Traditionalists who are cocooned in the past are always fearful of the bold, risk-taking adventure of the present. As Gaelic speakers we have to adopt new strategies for the survival of our language in a changing society, adapt ourselves to the multiple cultural realities around us. All the recent statistical studies show that the Gaeltacht, the historical heartland of Gaelic, is in a state of decline. Personally, I'm inclined nowadays to see the Gaeltacht as a fragmented entity, geographically dispersed across the globe. It is wherever people come together to speak Gaelic – a gay bar in Greenwich Village, a shopping mall in Sydney, a *sean-nós* class in Monte Carlo, a St John's Night in Hong Kong.

Change is, of course, a crucial aspect of life. We live in a world of flux and ferment where "being" is eternally in a state of "becoming". Consequently culture is never a fixed, immutable entity, something finished once and for all that we inherit and preserve. The notion that Gaelic culture stands motionless in time, perfectly transfixed in the past, is a common belief in our country. I'm not at all interested in that myopic view of culture. I'm interested in the creative and transformative possibilities of culture; its ability to renew itself, to develop and evolve. To be fluid and dynamic, futuristic and forward-looking. Too often we become mesmerised by the past instead of paying attention to the present. It's like driving a car and looking in the rear-view mirror instead of out the windscreen. A deadly practice.

Cloich Cheann Fhaola where I live is both a parish of the past and a place in the future. We no longer live in pastoral seclusion. All households are now multi-channel receivers. As a result, there are inter-cultural exchanges going on in every sitting room. The outside world, whether we like it or not, seeps into our consciousness and conditions our outlook. The storytellers of my youth, those keepers of knowledge, those dispensers of folk wisdom, have been replaced by mechanised information. These days children surf the Net, play video games, commune with technology. That vital human link has become obsolete. We now live in a global Cloich Cheann Fhaola. Every day other cultures collide and comingle with us. "Controlled horizons", to use Joseph Campbell's phrase, are a thing of the past. I read somewhere that in 1983 some members of the Tuareg, a migratory tribe in the Sahara, postponed their annual migration for a week because they didn't want to miss the last episode of *Dallas*. The people of

Cloich Cheann Fhaola were similarly bewitched by the deadly charms of JR Ewing Jr.

In a poem called "The Errigal Road", John Montague has these lines: "All around shards of a lost tradition / Soon all our shared landscape will be effaced." The most challenging cultural issue for us in Cloich Cheann Fhaola is how to preserve our native language. We, like all peripheral cultures, are in danger of being absorbed into the amorphous mass of Anglo-American culture that sweeps and swells across the world. At present what makes us distinct and different is that we have our own language. Gaelic gives us a native viewpoint. It's our own window onto the world. Gaelic is still spoken by a considerable amount of people in this area but its longevity as the local community language is in doubt. English is becoming more and more the preferred language of the youth of the locality. Nevertheless, a great effort is being made at present to support and sustain the language. "Pleanáil Teanga", a state sponsored initiative to fund, strengthen and promote social and cultural language activities is doing tremendous work in the parish. Under the present leadership of Caitlín Ní Bhroin, a language officer with fertile ideas and imaginative flair, this pioneering venture is finding new ways to engage people in language awareness and as a result bring about a more favourable social attitude to speaking Irish. Admittedly, the Irish spoken by my own generation is not as syntactically elaborate or as stylishly elegant as that spoken by the previous generation. Our Irish is much coloured by borrowings from English. English insinuates itself into our speech. It infiltrates our syntax. It wiggles itself around our words. Our Irish is weakened by dilution. However, its lack of purity is neither here nor there. Our real challenge is to ensure its continuation. This requires a positive response from parents. So much of what we are is transmitted through our language. It would be a great loss to lose that native repository, that storehouse of the Gaelic experience. If we abandon Irish we renounce a part of ourselves. We also dispossess those that are yet to come.

At present we are experiencing convulsions of change in our society, a shifting of boundaries and reshaping of identities. With the increased migration to our shores in recent years we are living now in a state of cultural multiplicity. A time of wandering borders and an overlapping of cultures where it is no longer credible to believe in a single unified identity. Making claims for a pure identity can, as we know too well, create an aggressive polarity between people and lead to a vicious politics of intolerance.

Until recently the feet of many Chinese girls were bound up horrendously to hinder their natural growth. A deeply ingrained cultural perception led to the belief that deformed feet were objects of exquisite beauty. Likewise, living exclusively within a particular ethnic identity can lead to a distorted condition of the mind that skews the vision and wraps the outlook. It is necessary to break out of these imposed constructs and establish more relaxed parameters for ourselves. Personally I'm delighted by this rainbow river of culture that is sweeping through our lives here in Ireland now. We never before experienced such creeds, such languages, such colours in our midst. It is healthy to open up to the uniqueness and the strangeness of these cultures. We will be enriched by their differences, their diversity, their ethnic perspectives.

20

From my upstairs window I'm looking out at Errigal. It's clear and bright in the Maytime sunshine. Today its chiselled face has a purity of outline that even I, who have no skill in drawing or in painting could perhaps capture with pen and ink.

A splurge of yellow gorse and a hawthorn in a white bridal dress fills the foreground. The rarefied blue of a holiday-brochure sky gives the whole scene a sense of ease and contentment.

The silky vellum of the hawthorn blossoms makes me want to write. The task of the artist according to Ibsen is to make clear to himself and thereby to others the temporal and the eternal questions. In other words to cast light on the human condition.

We live in unsettling times; war, famine, the large scale displacement of people, a looming climate catastrophe, an eroding of tolerant, humane values by oppressive regimes.

More than ever, we need to hear voices of wisdom: and not the ego-rants of Trump and his like. We need to hear sound judicious words imbued with a generosity of Spirit and a breath of vision. We need to attune ourselves to the redemptive power of Music – to the affirmative power of Poetry. We need to have an ear to the ground. We need to turn a new leaf.

This is also my book-room. While sitting here admiring the view of Errigal from my window I usually read. Today I pick up Derek Jarman's *A Dungeness Notebook*, a book that never fails to inspire me.

It's an uplifting compendium of diary notes, poems and prose pieces that narrates his life at Prospect Cottage, a fisherman's hut on the sea-shingle at Dungeness that he bought in 1986 at the onset of his HIV diagnosis.

Despite his illness and the palpable threat of death that came with HIV infection in the early days of the AIDS crisis, Derek Jarman found a sustaining energy in the compelling bleakness of Dungeness. For most people, threatened with such an unpromising fate, Dungeness for them would be a grey shore of shipwrecked hopes.

For Derek Jarman it was a haven of possibilities. It became the heartland of his inspiration. With a bold, courageous vision he created a unique garden at Prospect Cottage. He coaxed a hardy marine habitat into being where there was nothing but bare stubborn shingle.

In spite of the lack of soil, the encroachment of tidal overflows, and the assault of brutal salt-winds, he managed to turn this unyielding stony shingle into a place of growth and bloom. A flowering miracle!

Integrated into this rare garden of marine plants and shrubs are the beached objects that he assiduously collected. He found in this retch of debris that the sea belched forth objects of interest. With his imaginative flair he turned these found objects into provocative sculptural features in his garden.

A garden without walls, fences or boundaries, open to the briny tumult of the sea, and to the ravages of stormy nights and wind-scoured days.

How wonderfully daring the enterprise was and still is for it has outlived its creator; a triumph of endurance, to become a source of solace and wonder to those who pilgrim to this revered site.

Derek Jarman is an important ecological voice, a contemplative ecologist who connects us in his writings to the elemental and the sacred.

This *Dungeness Notebook* that I'm reading contains candid autobiographical fragments, plant lore and lively reflections. I'm captivated by the expressive charm of his style; his eye for the sensuous and the significant detail and his luminous moments of insight.

Someone asserted that Patrick Kavanagh was a great poet because he had a fervent belief that what happened in his own fields was both local and universal.

Like Kavanagh, Jarman is grounded in one small area in Dungeness and in his writings he reveals it over and over, a devoted exploration.

This close observation of place, as in many of Kavangh's poems, oftentimes borders on the mystical.

It reminds me also of Morandi, the Italian artist who painted obsessively the view from his window. A small area endlessly examined, looked into, probed. The garden, the road to the village, the hills beyond. All painted in stilled delight.

Derek Jarman has the same consuming, spellbound vision as he moves about exploring the boundlessness of his small space; his cottage, his garden, his bit of sea shore. Before his own light was extinguished he cast a permanent radiance over the grey shingle of Dungeness. It reminds me that my own compulsive meanderings around Errigal are not dissimilar in nature to Morandi's view from the window or Jarman's ponderings in Prospect Cottage.

21

I'm standing on Ard na Míne overlooking Loch an Ghainimh. Trailing puffs of white flossy clouds dot the sky. Errigal is a pale misty blue mountain. It's so close it seems as if I could touch it.

Clouds, blue mountain, September light; it could well be a Paul Henry painting that I'm seeing. That strange, unearthly Irish light that you only get in the West of Ireland is shed over a landscape that is incised and lacerated from years of turf cutting. The light this evening is like some heavenly balm that soothes all that has been cut-up, sliced, scarred and left raw.

I remember being here on a magical September evening of clouds, mist and light with my friend Colin Peck. Sadly, Colin has passed away. He died, a vigorous middle-aged man, from a fatal heart attack at Preehan House, his homeplace on the outskirts of Derry City.

There is no accounting for the randomness of Death and the ceaseless shifting of all that we cherish and hold dear. Our ephemeral human life is made more stark when confronted by these age-old, enduring mountains. Each of us is only a casual moment of chance in the overall course of things. Fortunately the imagination gives us the amplitude and the ability to live beyond ourselves, to inhabit the past, to enlarge the present and to enact the future.

Colin loved these bog lakes, the shifting light, the stone-walled lanes and fields and the unhurried life of our hillside communities. He found it restorative to come here and enjoy this upland calm.

Colin didn't do things by half. How could he? He was born with that headlong, high-spirited, irrepressible dash. He flung himself into life with verve, style and spirit. He gave of himself wholly and willingly.

He died of a massive heart attack. Colin didn't and couldn't do anything in a half-hearted way. I like to think that it was a massive surge of life that took him into the Evermore. A slow, sickly trickle into Eternity would have dispirited him.

Colin was Peck by name but certainly not by nature. He didn't peck at things. No! He bit right into that delicious, mouth-watering apple of knowledge. He knew that it was the only sustainable way to wisdom.

Once I said to him, jokingly of course, "Only seven deadly sins. How restricting." He laughed that lovely tinkling laugh of his and said: "What we need is not to harp on about Sin but to point up the importance of Pleasure. To even out the effects of the Seven Deadly Sins we need to have at least a hundred canonically approved Pleasures." Colin believed that we shouldn't make a ceremony of death out of the miracle of life. How to catch the pace of his life, the tempo of his excitements! His war-zone days in Afghanistan,

Chechnya, Moscow with his brother Rory, that bold swashbuckling Frontline cameraman; the huge task of taking on the restoration and maintenance of a stately home; and not least among his gritty feats, fatherhood, and its incumbent responsibilities.

Enough to say that Colin responded to life and its challenges with courage, spirit and resolve.

He had the indoor charm and manners of a most gracious host and the outdoor enthusiasms of a cultured, Victorian country gentleman. He was the kind of man who allowed wild flowers, windswept clouds and West Donegal into his life. And he was a connoisseur of mushrooms! And a gourmet of fresh air.

I remember being with him one evening on a magical mushroom trip. No, we weren't looking for the tripping variety, just the good edible types but we didn't have to. In Colin's company it was a sweet, vivid, spaced-out trip anyway.

And I wish I could say that Death has no Dominion. But it has. It leaves us bereft and bewildered.

The death of a loved one is incised in the guts of the living.

The space that Colin occupied so graciously, so vibrantly, so meaningfully is empty.

That Domain where he thrived is now silent. And that silence, for all of us who knew and loved him, looms large and fathomless. A chasm.

Before I return home I stand facing Errigal and in memory of Colin. I offer up a prayer, "trembling with light, coarse with earth, murmuring with water and with wind." Those lines are burrowed from a poem by Eugenio de Andrade, a Portuguese poet whose work enthralls me.

22

The Droim Dubh between Loch An Ghainimh and Loch Altan is a big stretch of bogland close to where I live in Mín an Leá. It lies at the Errigal end of an expanse of brown brindled moorland called Cnoc na Bealtaine.

To some these vast acreages of boglands are bleak, lonely, inhospitable places but to me they are havens of peace and wonder far from the rush-hour jostle and the snarling traffic of towns and cities.

I don't mind at all the slosh and squelch of tramping through these spongy bogs. There's so much going on at my feet that engages my attention; the vegetal life that characterises the place.

I'm very fond of the bog myrtle, a bushy grey green shrub that carries a most delicate fragrance in its leaves. When you rub them between your fingers it releases a subtle aroma that is not unlike the smell of eucalyptus. I could binge on it. The sundew is another plant that always catches my attention. It's one of those spooky carnivorous entities, and although a plant, feeds on flesh. It has a sticky mess on its tentacles which traps small insects and then ingests them in this fluid that is full of enzymes. The sundew needs these fleshy nutrients, it seems, as a mineral supplement which it cannot obtain in the bog-soil.

The orchids with their soft purple opulence and their pagoda-like build are a joy to behold. Likewise the silky white plantations of bog-cotton shimmering in the sun; the purple and pale lavender radiance of August – blooming heather as it glows aura-like across these bogs is a blessing to see. Later when the deer grass and the bog asphodel commingle to give these moorlands the russet-red tinge of late autumn, it is for me that time of year when they are at their most delicately beautiful.

A friend who is knowledgeable in these matters told me once that some of the alpine plants, the lichens, the mosses, the saxifrages that thrive higher up the mountain, survived the glacial crush and wipe-out of the last ice age. This tenacity to survive and live on through cataclysmic ruin is both astonishing to me and uplifting. They, like our own human species, came through those ice-hard eras to seed anew and to flourish in more temperate times.

Recently, I heard a mother scowling her daughter: "Don't sit there and vegetate." And I thought how inappropriate and ill-suited the use of the word "vegatate" appeared to be. Although a plant is stationary above ground it has a busy, sinewy life underground, stretching through the soil in search of nourishment and then conserving the food in its larder of roots. Vegetative in that sense is not a negative act but an active one. The young girl in her pensive mood was more than likely rooting in her mind for answers, for significance, for sustenance.

The Droim Dubh was opened up during the Second World War for its abundance of turf. Because of the war the usual supply of coal was not getting into the country. In this emergency the government set in motion large-scale turf-cutting to satisfy domestic needs, especially those of city dwellers who until then depended on coal.

The wartime summers were busy here on the Droim Dubh. Young and old were wage-earners at the turf-saving. It was an unhoped-for income at a time when a war raged abroad. The back-bending slog of saving turf was hard but the craic was mighty, my father told me. The turf was carted to Caiseal na gCorr station and then carried by train to Dublin where it was stacked in the Phoenix Park and from there it was distributed to Dublin households.

It's November now and this bog after a busy summer and autumn of growth and blossoming is slowing down and taking its winter rest. A dusky grey, heavy-eyed look spreads across its features as it nods off and conserves its energies for a spring awakening.

I'm sitting on a plush pile of velvety yellow and mauve moss, enjoying my own private silence as the day darkens and cloud shadows flit across the hillsides. Just now an arrowhead of wild geese dipped and honked and passed over Errigal. And suddenly in my memory I'm lying in bed listening to these same flapping wings and that eerie wheeling cry across the night-skies of my childhood. For a moment I was that child again wishing to travel with these airy beings to far-flung places of wonder, to imaginary lands beyond the bounds of the everyday. In this childish reverie the patches of scree on Achla Mór become the maps of fabulous domains.

While in that blissful state of innocence I stroke a stone that is shaggy with lichen. It purred.

At Loch an Ghainimh on my way back home, a fox, ears alert, darts across my path and disappears, blending in with the red-brown bog.

FOX

I come in the darkness.
My stealth is my wealth.
I'm a prowler, a croucher.
I stalk the night, I plunder.

In the autumn I cover
These wild boglands
Above Loch an Ghainimh
With the red sedge of my tail.

23

It's mid-November. A soft breezy wind blows from Gleann Tornáin. Loch an Troisc is a corrugated sheet of grey. I'm walking on the old railway line past the lake and up a steep hummocky slope to the top of An Trosc Ghlas.

The weather is still mild, even a little balmy at times and as yet no trace of frost at night. On my way here from Mín an Leá I noticed a rowan tree standing stock still like a footman, its red-berry livery still spick-and-span even this late in the season. I come across the dainty yellow bird's-foot trefoil, the trailing tormentil and the occasional pale lavender orchid still lingering on after their summer showing. The gorse is burgeoning again and in some cases where it has erupted in yellow I inhale its sweet coconut fragrance.

A cascade of rainclouds tumbles down the mountainsides from Errigal across the Achlas to Muckish but by a lucky chance it remains dry on top of An Trosc Ghlas. Gradually this cloud surge lifts up and moves out to sea. Now I have a clear view of Errigal except for a wispy helix-shaped cloud hovering on its shoulder. I can see a group of brightly-clad climbers emerge out of this vapoury wonder as if from a spaceship and make their way to the top.

An Trosc Ghlas is a hill full of nooks and crannies. My father used to call it Cnoc an Radharc, the hill with a view and in the past it was a favourite spot for courting couples. I can well imagine the giddy delight of a tryst on this hill of sights and the breathless panoramic promises that were made, and alas, never kept.

As the wind sighs around the sheltered nook where I'm sitting it brings to my mind the sibilant note of mourning that you find in most of our love poems, that keen of loss. Gaelic poetry has always known how to manipulate the vowels of sorrow.

I'm looking down at Mín na Craoibhe snug in its patchwork of fields, each one of them fluent in its own dialect of green. Diane Ní Chanainn, whose father comes from Mín na Craoibhe is one of my favourite sean-nós singers. In her singing she is faithful to the grace and verve of these old songs, to their words and airs. But she also casts her own inimitable spell of enchantment over all of them.

I love these sean-nós songs with their elaborate artistry; their intricate textures of language, their rich, vibrant melodies, their mournful and yet passionate themes. They are, I believe, authentic expressions of the Gaelic Psyche. What I most like, and indeed envy about these song lyrics is their delicate vowel harmonies, the Gaelic counterpart of rhyme, I suppose. For a long time these songs of the people were considered to be sub-literary, but now, a whole new generation of knowledgeable and devoted scholars and musicologists have shown that this genre is highly stylised and elaborate in syntax and in sound. Professor Lillis Ó Laoire, one of the most eminent and wide-ranging scholars of the Gaelic song tradition is my next-door neighbour in Mín an Leá. He is also one of the most esteemed and expressive sean-nós singers of his generation and an inspiring mentor to a younger generation.

My friend, Máire Ní Choilm, who comes with me from time to time on these hill walks is also a celebrated sean-nós singer. She herself is highly informed about the song tradition and that, coupled with the individual genius of her voice, enables her to bring these songs alive in a dynamically fresh, and yet, timeless way.

This wilderness around Loch An Troisc is a suitable abode for an anchorite. Who knows, it may have been so in ancient times. In a far-off era it was a greenwood, the tree stumps are still visible. By all accounts the Golden Age of monasticism and of hermitism coincided with a period of gradual warming in Ireland. The weather was mostly benign and you could live an outdoor life of forageing. Living in a sunny clime, sustained by nature's bounty of berries, nuts and fish; surrounded by birdsong and the company of Earth's little creatures is the lyrical theme of much early Irish nature poetry. It's a literature imbued with a green sense of awe at the Creation and one that has much to enlighten us in the here and now of global warming and its cumulative horrors.

As I walk back home I'm thankful for the meditative rhythms of walking and how it calms the mind and eases stress.

A blackbird sings a twilight song in a crab-apple tree below Wright's house.

24

In stormy weather I like to walk on exposed paths above Loch An Ghainimh. Daunting it may be but it's also invigorating. The slap of rain and the whip of wind is bracing. And it always brightens up, even momentarily, and I get a chance to smooch with the light. The joy of our hill climate is the mercurial shifts of weather that we get. Today we could have the rarefied blue of a holiday brochure sky. Tomorrow a damp newspaper of grey cloud may hang over everything. I like these sudden shifts from bright to bleak.

This is a treeless, exposed ridge. In fact the whole mountainscape where I live is treeless except in Gleann Tornáin and Na Learacha where the government planted fast growing conifers. I'm not at all in favour of these one-species forests that are grown as cash crops. Unlike our native woodlands (there are so few of them left in Donegal) with their rich biodiversity of plants and birds, these commercially grown ventures give me the impression of being sour, soulless places. In these places the forest floor is usually without life; a yellowing spiky mat that smothers growth. This is so different from the life-enhancing habitats of our native woodlands where in spring lovely sprays of wood anemone and bluebells adorn their floors. In summer the pink cuckoo flower flourishes and festoons of honeysuckle sweeten the air.

Birdlife abounds and these woods ring out their green cantatas of song. My friend, Sean Ó Gaoithín, who is the head gardener at Glenveigh Castle, has written beautifully and perceptively about our native woodlands in Donegal. His discerning talks have made me a hugger of oaks and a cuddler of birches.

Today in this overcast weather, this Droim is a sulky expanse of bog. How glib we are to give these landscapes emotional traits. They exist in their own wild sphere beyond the human, and yet, they share with us a need to live; to breathe, and to propagate. I admire their tenacity to live. I have often noticed how after a heath fire, when all the vegetation is burnt black, this charred landscape manages to sprout again with renewed vigour. Evidently given half a chance, the will to live is strong and encoded in all seed.

A dense mist descends and the countryside around me seems to contract.

I'm in a veiled world of shimmers, of diffused unsteady light. There are no landmarks. Errigal is obscured in cloud. I'm both charmed and repelled by this diminution of my world.

Later, on the hill road, I met a man who told me that the mist had left him bewildered. Loosing sense of familiar landmarks was like a sudden mental aberration. For a while he found himself astray in a terra incognito of the mind where he had no bearings, no sense of direction. The course he did in orientation was of no earthly use in those unmapped domains. He was all right now, he said. He could see a clear path ahead. He thanked me for walking with him to the end of the road.

As I made my own way home it occurred to me that the mystic poets, the likes of Rumi, Kabir, Walt Whitman, St John of the Cross did navigate the terra incognito of the mind. They are the pathfinders, the true pioneers of inner travel.

Before I reached home the mist began to rise, Errigal like an oracle spoke in clouds.

25

If the weather is good, I often sit at a bench in my garden and write, facing Errigal. I'm lucky to have this lovely uplifting presence in front of me as I write or potter about in the garden. I think of Derek Jarman in his garden at Dungeness with the grey, ominous hulk of a nuclear reactor constantly within sight. He endured it and carried on, re-seeing the world anew each day despite that foreboding presence.

For years he endured the punishing effects of HIV but through all that terrible suffering he still continued to be actively creative as an audacious film-maker, a bold chronicler of a deadly plague, a daring painter and a diligent, undaunted gardener who made a stony shingle at Dungeness into an oasis of bloom. He died in 1994 of AIDS-related complications. I admire his dashing, buoyed-up courage in the face of a tragic fate. For me he is Saint Derek of Dungeness, a man of gay and noble convictions who did not make a ceremony of death out of the miracle of life.

Derek's garden in Dungeness is an open one but I had to fence mine off to safeguard my shrubs and plants, from roaming sheep. Some farmers ignore boundaries and let their flock graze freely on their neighbours' unfenced land. So far I have avoided a rampage of sheep but they have their wiles and dodges to slip under fences and to bound over walls. They always have their eye on the greenery. All of us who are engaged in gardening know how enriching the activity is; being in contact with the Earth, appreciating its generosity and its nurturing abilities. Blessed are they who are in touch with roots and mulch and seeds. Blessed are they who are attuned to seasonal growth and decay. Blessed are they who cherish the soil.

This little garden in flower, looking up towards Errigal is my idea of Eden. It's controlled neither by design, style or custom. It has its own fancy-free catalogue of plants; its own random élan of colour. Frivolous shades of pink, delirious reds and flagrant blues give it a saucy vividness. Some people impose a severe etiquette of colour on their gardens but I'm the one for the wanton and the rampant.

Over the past couple of years I have lived in a glorious "bee-loud glade" throughout the summer months because of an abundance of meadow flowers in my garden: cornflowers, marigolds, flowering flax, larkspur, love-in-a-mist, vipers bugloss, Californian poppies. This honey-fuelled litany of flowers is one of my Earth prayers.

Gardening for me is a romantic pursuit in the sense that I spend days doting on the sweet Williams, ogling the pansies, and having intrigues among the asters.

I cruise along the herbaceous borders and enjoy a tryst in the shrubbery, with a wild flower.

I have no doubt but that Derek Jarman would approve of the levity.

This is peace, to sit here in the garden, write and watch the day inscribe its own passages of light on Errigal.

26

It's December and the mountains are coated in snow. Errigal, like an Old Testament Patriarch, wears a long shimmering robe of white and on its cheeks, a flowing beard of cloud. I stand at my upstairs window for a long time gazing up at it in awe.

These mornings I'm awakened early by the glow of snow. I'm keen to live in the present.

Too many people live life as if it were a rehearsal, a try-out, a dry run for the real thing, the authentic life to come further down the road.

The most keenly lived life is, I believe, the one in which the door of the heart is always open to receive the present. Too many people keep their focus narrow, their windows of wonder curtained tight by habit and conformity. They shun the heady options of the present. The urgency of the moment, the shock of the now is more potent to me than the promise of the future. The spirited vibrancy of the here-and-now is what excites me.

"Jump into experience while you are alive", Kabir, the Indian mystic poet urged his followers.

I believe in beginning my walks anew each day, and in having regular upsurges of wonder. When we are no longer in awe of the creation we suffer spiritual stagnation. Too often grown-ups waste away in bored solitude within themselves without ever experiencing that stir of wonder that transforms the mind and makes us visionaries of the real.

Here at Loch an Ghainimh is a good place for snow viewing. The snowy peaks of Mucais, the Achlas and Errigal make a beautiful backdrop to the fiery bronze of the winter bogs.

In the bright frosty air a wedge of wild geese honk their way towards Dunlewey. A lone duck ripples the lake water. Whorled ropes of ice stretch between rocks. On the path down to the lake I see a delicate tracery of bird tracts scrawled across the snow like Chinese ideograms. Or perhaps they are bird haikus scrolled expertly on this white parchment. The potholes of scummy water on the road have now become frosted panels of stained glass. As the afternoon sun falls across the hills the strong glare of frosty snow gleams and scintillates, a treasure trove of crystals.

The light is fading as I return home. The shadowed hills give off a rosy afterglow and Errigal still holds its hypnotic brilliance. A sharp bite in the December air prompts this haiku:

> Chill December air —
> the red glow of holly
> warms my kitchen.

Later I go out for a breath of fresh air. It's a clear, crisp, starlight night. Under a full moon this world of snow gives off a lovely soft shimmer. It's a night in white satin. A touch of frost enlivens the air and I feel alive to the beat and thump of my own being. It's so still and beautiful. It reminds me of the floating world of Japanese woodblock prints. In its mood, this snow world of Mín an Leá with its pale misty loveliness could be a Hokusai or a Hiroshige print.

And there is Errigal, my own Fujiyama, my muse mountain resplendent in the night, beaming down at me.

ERRIGAL:
A SUITE OF POEMS

The English translations of the following
15 Irish-language poems begin on page 219.

AN tEARAGAIL: MACHNAMH

1

Ní labhrann tú
ach go hannamh
agus tú ar do mharana,
a ghúrú an cheana.

Rúnfhocal amháin
ó sheal go seal
á thíolacadh agat
as do bhéal.

Carraig d'fhocal,
tromchiallach.
Ábhar machnaimh,
rúndiamhrach.

Ní labhrann tú
ach go hannamh.
Sin an fáth a bhfuil
an fraoch ag fás

sa spás idir d'fhocail.

2

Is tú ár laoch
i mbearna na gaoithe,
ar ngaiscíoch dásachtach
i mbéal na bruíne.

Seasmhach, dílis, móruchtúil,
ár gcosaint, a dhíograis,
ó ruathar stoirme,
ó anfa geimhridh.

Ár gcuradh réidh,
sciath ghealaí i do dheis
sleá gréine i do chlé.

I do cholgsheasamh
agus faoi riastradh,
ní baol dúinn an anachain,

agus tú sa bhearna bhaoil,
a fhir ghnímh,
a Mhic an Earagail.

3

Tá tú i ngrá
leis an fharraige
cé nár mhaith leat é a rá;
an fharraige luascach, líofa, lúth,
a labhrann leat gach lá
le fuaim bhinn na dtonn.
Tá tú faoi gheasa
ag a súile glasa luainneacha,
ag a cosa geala lúbacha,
ag a hanáil ghoirt.
De shíor tá tú ag éisteacht
lena cuid rachtanna cainte,
lena cuid taomanna goil.
Níl tarraingt d'anála ionat
nuair a nochtann sí
a mása móra mara
amuigh ansiúd i mbéal Thoraí.
Tá tú i ngrá leis an fharraige
is beidh go brách,
ach anseo tá tú i bhfód
go domhain is go daingean
is ní aistreoidh tú ariamh
léithe siar sa ród.

4

Chan ionann agus an fharraige
atá go huile ina boige,
sobhogtha agus spreagtha
ina dearcadh, ina cleachtadh,
í tógtha suas le taisteal
na gcríocha, seal thíos, seal thuas.

Tá tusa trom ionat féin,
i gcónaí ag iompar meáchain.
Righin i do mheon agus righin
i do mheabhair, níor chleacht tú
an teacht agus an t-imeacht.
Tá tú cruaidh, dobhogtha i do dhóigh.

Ach lá éigin níos faide
anonn, déanfaidh an fharraige
an ball bog a aimsiú ionat,
nuair a thiocfaidh sí i dtír,
ag maidhmeadh a coirp tharat
go tiarnasach, gealghlórach.

5

Nár mhéanar
dá mbeinn ag cur fúm
ar feadh mo shaoil
i do dhíseartán fraoigh,
ar do shleasa gaothrite
ar do bheanna grianlasta,
do do dhreapadh gach lá
de choiscéim chneasta.

Is tú an staighre chun na spéire,
dréimire na gréine.
Sa tsolas ar do bharr
d'aimseoinn mé féin,
is bheadh tuigbheáil agam
nach dtig ó shleachta suadh
ach ó ghaoth ag teacht
de dhroim sneachta,

oíche sa Mhárta rua
is ó shú bog na bhfraochóg
i bhfómhar na smear.
Bheinn ag adhradh na ndúl
is an mhaidin óg
ag cur maise ort

is do do mhóradh
os comhair mo dhá shúil.

Nár mhéanar
ealú ó gheimhle an tsaoil,
ceangal na gcúig gcaol
a scaoileadh saor, liú
dúshláin a chur asam
ar do bhuaic gealaí,
ar do bheanna baoil.

Dálta Han Shan
an t-oilithreach dána
a chaith a shaol thuas
ar an tSliabh Fhuar,
an file beoshúileach,
fiánta, fadfhulangach,
á shaoradh féin go buan
sna scamaill bhána.

6

Tá an fharraige de shíor ag caint,
ag scaipeadh scéalta.

Tá tusa go buan i do thost,
ag meabhrú ar néalta.

7

Dá labharfá thusa ar an éigse
bheadh do chuid cainte lán de chloch-thuigse.

8

Inniu baineadh
soir asam
sa Mhám
idir tú féin
agus an Cnoc Glas.
Bhí mé i gcéin
agus as m'am.
Chonacthas domh go raibh
gairdín criosantamam
amuigh i mbláth
faoi do scáth,
go raibh coillidh
crann silíní
ag craobhú ar do bheanna,
go raibh aeráid na Seapáine
ag cur aoibhe ort is gnaoi,
go raibh Mín na Craoibhe
i gcroílár Kyoto,
go raibh bean i gKimono
ag umhlú duit go béasach.

Mura raibh ann ach mearbhall ama
a shaobh mé, is cuma.
Chonaic mé Hokusai, an saoi,
agus é ar a ghlúine d'adhradh
a Earagail, a Fujiyama.

9

As tinidh thús an tsaoil
a cruthaíodh thú.

Tá beo den tinidh sin
ag dó ionat i dtólamh,
an choigilt i do chuid carraigeacha,
an laom i do chuid leacacha.

Tá an spréach sin ag feitheamh
ar lá na cinniúna
nuair a bhrúchtfaidh sé
as do chlocha giniúna,
ina bhladhm lasrach,
ina chraos mhillteach.

As tinidh a cruthaíodh thú
I dtinidh a chaillfear thú.

10

Is réidh agat é!
bhí tú ann romhainn,
beidh tú ann inár ndiaidh.

11

As gríos na giniúna
a fáisceadh thú,
an t-oighear a mhúnlaigh thú,
an ghaoth is an ghrian
a shnoigh thú,
an sneachta is an síon
a chuir snas ort,
an fraoch a chuir snua ionat,
an caonach a chuir éideadh ort,
an raideog a chumhraigh thú,
an ceannbhán a d'fhág féasóg ort,
an fhuiseog a thug ceol duit,
an nádúr a thug buanaíocht duit,
an nádúraí, an créatúr díomuan,
a thugann ómós duit.

12

An cuimhneach leat
na glúnta urramacha
a chaith a mbeatha
ag saothrú is ag síolrú
i dtráth agus in antráth
anseo faoi do scáth?

Nó ar imigh siad
na fir úd agus na mná
a d'fhéach suas ort
go hómósach gach lá,
ar imigh siad go brách
as annálacha do chuimhne?

An caill duit an duine?

13

Níl sliocht ar bith ort,
mo dhálta féin, a chroí,
ach amháin an saothar seo
le do thaobh, na cnuasaigh
cloch seo, dánta crua
a tháinig asat le dua.

Tá an chloch ghréine
ag lonrú go líofa
i do chuid dánta molta;
an t-eibhear tréan
ag neartú do chaointe;
an chloch aoil
géar i do chuid aortha.

Tá mé in éad leo.
Buanóidh siad
nuair atá mo chuidse
imithe ina gceo.

14

Tráthnóna samhraidh
is mé ag siúl an tsléibhe
bíonn tú romham
i linnte portaigh,
beag agus gnaíúil
amhail is go dtiocfadh liom
breith ort agus barróg
a thabhairt duit, a dhuine chléibh.

15

Shiúil mé thú i gcéimeanna miona,
gach malaidh is mullach, gach log is learg,
gach binn shíon-nite, gach droim grianlite.
Dhearc mé go cruinn a raibh ag fás ort go gleoite,
do chuid lusanna fiáine is do chuid luibheanna íce.

Chonaic mé thú i bhfallaing liathbhán an Mhárta
agus i mbréidín fraoigh an fhómhair.
Chonaic mé thú i gclóca gréine na Bealtaine
is i mbáine shíodúil an Eanáir
ach dá mhéad a dhearcaim thú is lú

d'aithne is d'eolas a chuirim ort, a rún,
ach sin dán an té atá faoi do gheasa diamhra.

MOUNT ERRIGAL

1

Rarely
do you speak
wrapped in contemplation
guru of my adoration.

Once in a while
a *koan* might slip
from your mouth
as a gift.

Your word is a rock
of weight,
a mystery
to meditate.

Rarely
do you speak
which is why
heather breaks out

in the space between your words.

Translated by Gabriel Rosenstock

2

You are our warrior
in the gap of the wind,
our daring champion

Faithful, steadfast, stout of heart,
our shelter, our eager
guard against skirmishing storms,
against winter's blitzkrieg.

Our imperturbable hero,
in your left hand a lunar shield
a blade of sunlight in your right.

When your hackles rise
in the frenzy of battle
tempests do not threaten us

While you man the gap of danger,
you of high deeds and lineage,
Errigal, Son of Errigal.

Translated by Paddy Bushe

3

You are in love
with the sea
but loathe to say it;
the fluent, sinewy, swaying sea
who every day speaks to you
in the sweet utterance of waves.
You are entranced
by her glittering green eyes,
her lithe white legs,
her briny breath.
You never tire of listening
to her streams of talk,
to her paroxysms of weeping.
There is a catch in your breath
when she bares those heaving buttocks
far out in Tory Sound.
You are in love with the sea,
and always will be,
but you are anchored here
deep down beyond budging,
with not a ghost of a chance
you'll go roving out with her.

Translated by Paddy Bushe

4

Not at all like the sea
all downy and malleable,
flexible and tensile
in her outlook, her habits,
absorbed in exploring
margins, up down and all over.

You are weighty in yourself
always bearing some load.
Unmoving in temperament
in thought, you were never into
non-stop arrivals and departures.
Your ways are steadfast, rooted.

But some fine day in the far
future, the sea will nuzzle out
your soft spot, your weak point,
when she makes landfall,
inundating her body around you,
dominating with wild bright cries.

5

What a dream it is
to imagine spending
the whole rest of my life
in your heathery hermitage,
on your wind-ridden slopes
around your sunlit peaks
ascending you each day
with compassionate footsteps.

You are the steps to the sky,
the ladder towards the sun.
In the light of your summit,
I would unearth myself,
and I would have awareness
not from the work of sages
but from a wind whistling
from the tops of snowy ridges

or in its wild March rages,
and from soft whortleberries
in their autumn juiciness.
I would pay homage to the elements
while the vestal morning virgin
garlanded and decked you
with votive respect
before my very eyes.

What a dream it is
to sever the world's fetters,
to free the manacles
on life and limbs, and to whoop
my defiance to the air
on your moonlit peak,
your hazardous heights.

Then to become Han Shan
pilgrim of high daring
exalting his whole life
on the eminence of Cold Mountain,
the wide-eyed poet,
shaman, ascetic,
setting himself forever free
into the white clouds.

6

The sea is a constant bubble of rumour,
mouth ajar!

You are lofty in eternal silence
contemplating the next star.

Translated by Gabriel Rosenstock

7

If you talk at all you talk to yourself alone,
poetry of stone.

Translated by Gabriel Rosenstock

8

Today
I went askew
in the Mám
between yourself
and Cnoc Glas.
Out of my dimensions
outside of time.
It appeared to me
that a garden of chrysanthemums
was blooming
in your shade,
and woods of
cherry trees
were branching out from your peaks,
the air of Japan
had wreathed you in smiles
and Mín na Craoibhe
was in the middle of Kyoto,
a woman in a kimono
bowing to you politely.
Was I momentarily duped?
It matters not.

The sage Hokusai was visible to me
on his knees in adoration —
Fuji-Errigal!

Translated by Gabriel Rosenstock

9

The primal conflagration
was your casting.

A glowing from that furnace
persists in your core
hoarded in your rocks
a seething in your slabs.

That ember awaits
the day of reckoning
when it will haemorrhage
from the stones of your begetting
in fiery inundation
voracious carnage.

Created in fire,
in fire you will perish.

Translated by Paddy Bushe

10

Fine and easy you have it!
here before us
still here after us.

11

You were wrung
from generative embers,
ice formed you,
wind and sun
sculpted you,
snow and storm
pelted you smooth,
heather made your skin glow,
moss clothed you,
bog myrtle perfumed you,
bog cotton downed your cheeks,
larks piped you music,
nature immortalised you,
and nature-lovers, poor mortal creatures,
venerate you.

Translated by Paddy Bushe

12

Do you remember them
those treasured generations
who spent their lives
slaving and sowing
good years and bad
here in your shadow?

Or were they erased,
those men and women
who raised their eyes to you
respectfully day after day,
were they erased irrevocably
from the annals of your memory?

Does human absence echo in you?

Translated by Paddy Bushe

13

You have no offspring,
like myself, dear heart,
but for this travail
beside you, these collections
of stones, poems hard won
after long labour.

The white quartz
gleams eloquently
in your poems of praise;
the unyielding granite
strengthens your keening;
limestone is the cutting
edge of your satire.

I begrudge them.
They will endure
when mine are misted
into impermanence.

Translated by Paddy Bushe

14

Summer evenings
when I walk the uplands
I see you looking at me
from small bog-pools,
handsome in miniature
so that I could circle
my two arms around you
and, friend of my heart, hug you.

Translated by Paddy Bushe

15

I walked you with small, intimate steps,
each slope and summit, each hump and hollow,
every wind-washed gable and sun-licked ridge.
I took precise stock of your lovely growing things,
your wildflowers and your herbs of healing.

I saw you in the thin grey cloak of March
and in the heathery tweed of autumn.
I saw you glowing in May's aureate mantle
and in the silken sheen of January,
but the more intense my gaze, the less

I know and understand of you, dear oracle,
ordained to fail, just, to catch your words.

Translated by Paddy Bushe

ERRIGAL:
NOTEBOOK MUSINGS

These are reflections and aphorisms that came to me on my Errigal walks. I find that the heightened rhythm of hill-walking informs this kind of thought. It activates the mind to think latterly and even loftily. Breathing has a lot to do with it too. We take breathing for granted although it's what sustains us from the gasp of birth to the gulp of death.

Life is breath. Breath is life.

While walking I'm attentive to my breathing. I inhale deeply in and out through the nose. I let it spread slowly to each and every one of my limbs. I breathe for life. Breath is health. People suffer from ill health because they breathe shallowly. I'm convinced that this flow of energy to the lungs, to the blood, to the brain makes me more receptive to the possibility of Wisdom.

How to be wise, how to live in the stability of Truth is what we aspire to but seldom achieve.

How to become wise is the ultimate quest. A little vignette from James Thurber, that sage of humour, is insightful. The gist of the story, as I recall it, is a little boy asking his aged grandfather how he became wise.

"I'm wise", said the grandfather sagely, "because I have good judgement."

"But where do you get good judgement from, granda?"

"Well, you get good judgement from experience."

"But, granda, how you get experience?"

"O you get experience", replied the grandfather thoughtfully "from poor judgement."

We are not born into wisdom.

We gain it, painstaking mostly, from what we come up against and what we come through.

Wisdom is a clear distillation of experience.

It is serene understanding.

Errigal knows and a wise mountain never blows its knows.

Be a follower of your intuitions;
a disciple of your intelligence.

———

Have the strength to be meek;
the courage to be fearful.

———

We are dust but dust can coalesce and become
a flower, a mountain, a star, a lover.

———

Wealth loses its value but wisdom never depreciates.

A conditioned mind binds you.
A wondering mind allows you to be boundless.

———

Do not make a ceremony of death
out of the miracle of life.

———

Everything evolves,
everything dissolves,
change is the only constant in creation.

———

All is change.
Acknowledge what you are
and adjust to what you will become.

———

True humility lightens the mind.
Blind submission darkens it.

———

Detachment
is not indifference.
It's an awareness of impermanence.

Ventilate your mind.
Let the air of new ideas refresh it.

———

The ideal state of mind is
a mental repose that is relaxed but alert.
A composed calmness in the face
of hopelessness, in the face of death.
Knowing that all things, however precious,
change and pass away in the cycle of life.
Our real future is always in the present moment.

———

Life is fragile, life is fleeting.
We come and we go like clouds
scudding across the sky.
Happiness is when a cloud catches
sunlight and brightens.

———

In you the Earth yearns for the sky.
You are not a bird but imagination gives you wings.

Like the tree in winter shed your old convictions.
Let spring dress you in new beliefs.

———

Your thinking will only grow and flourish
if it's rooted in the earth of your experience.

———

A rose and a turd!
I praise them both.
They are signs of life.

———

You call him a fool because he wears
a nettle in his buttonhole.
I call him a poet.

———

Take your mind for a walk.
It needs daily exercise.

———

On my daily pilgrimage to the well,
the wild flowers are my wayside shrines.

We have to live outwardly
but grow inwardly.
Befriend your fears.

———

Keep the five seaports of your senses open,
many extraordinary cargoes will come your way.

———

Do not live in your past.
Visit it but only as a tourist.

———

Become a voyager in the universe of your imagination.
Discover a new inner geography of expansiveness.

———

The farmer's son knows that it's pointless
to plant potatoes in plastic bags
to keep the dirt out of their eyes.
Don't enclose your life in an ideology,
in dogma, in rigid patterns of belief.
Be open. Be attentive. Savour the joy of being.

Allow yourself to be touched by rapture,
to have moments of ecstasy.
Allow yourself, even momentarily,
to live in a time out of Time.

———

Be self-contained but not self-absorbed.
Have a conscience but better still have consciousness.

———

Beware the technology that ensnares
and the ideology that enslaves.

———

From time to time it's good to steer clear
of the commotion of words and to relish
the communion of silence.

———

Are you living in cellular confinement, a slave
to its incessant din and demands? Take a break.
Disconnect your connections.

Enlightenment means enlarging your consciousness.
Stilling the mind and strengthening the heart
are the two steps to contentment.
Get in contact with your own creative energies.
Have immaculate perceptions.

———

Call it what you will,
the life force,
the vital spark,
the breath of life,
the soul.
It is present in you as much as you are present in it.
It's what animates you.
Revere it.

———

Let the spirit of things reveal themselves to you.
Listen to the song of stones.
Be a See-r.
Take notice of ripples of light and the drift of mist.
Joy is portable. Carry it always.

Once a week be a bed of rumpled pleasures.
Avoid jaded kisses and shrivelled smiles.
Improvise. Be a slinky jazz tune.
Have a bawdy chat with a wild flower.

———

Creative energy is never wasted.
The ideas I failed to put in words are taking shape
in the smile of a child, in the jubilation of moths,
in the slither of a garden snail.

———

Worrying is the least useful of the mind's abilities,
fretting over something that has not happened,
agonising over an imaginary grief.
Worrying is worthless thinking.

———

If you insist on joining a creed, belong to one that
makes you think rather than one who thinks for you.

Ignorance creates fear and fear creates intolerance.
In grave times be inspired.
Vice can speak for itself!
It's virtue that needs a voice.
Think twice before you say nothing.

———

Walk the road to where reason ends
and then step out into wonder.

———

A mountain is the earth sighing for the infinite.
What is a tree but a green song!

———

Enjoy the little things in life.
Take in the scent of a rose and the smell of grass.
Sit in silence and experience patience.
Go on a hill trek up the stairs.
At sunset admire a frivolous shade of purple.
Treat yourself to a smile.

———

Don't let anger trail you like a thorny briar.
Don't let apathy hang over you like a whiff of decay.

ERRIGAL – AND ITS MISSING SACRED PAST

Brian Lacey

For a long time one of the most puzzling things for me about Errigal was that there were no traditional stories or lore about it: no folklore, no placelore / dinnseanchas, and no evident mythological associations. That was just not believable! Such an obvious physical feature – indeed such an awe-inspiring feature – must have attracted the speculations and imagination of those who had been living in its vicinity in pre-scientific times. Those ancient people must have developed stories about the mountain: how it came to exist; what sort of associations did it have with the gods and deities they believed dominated their world from the skies – skies that could be accessed, as it were, from the top of the mountain itself?

Whatever about before, based on the scatter of neolithic tombs to be found in the area just north of the mountain, we know that people were living within sight of it and near its base at least as far back as about 4,000 BC. Those people practiced agriculture and their livelihoods depended on whatever poured down on them from the sky: rain, sunshine, the changing temperature, the favours of the gods. It is inconceivable that this very visible and very unusually shaped mountain on their doorstep reaching up to that sky wasn't a central aspect of their everyday real environment and, perhaps more importantly, also of their spiritual culture. The mountain must have been held in awe, revered and venerated, perhaps even worshipped! Indeed, in 1937 the great Irish naturalist and antiquarian Robert Lloyd Praeger had commented:

> "Errigal ought to be a holy mountain, like Croagh Patrick; but it needs no association with a saint to make it an object of worship to all lovers of beauty."[1]

Undoubtedly Errigal *had* been such a holy mountain: but evidently the memory of those ancient associations had been lost or destroyed!

No! I came to the conclusion about ten years ago that something was wrong; there must have been such lore in the past but for some reason contrary to what we would normally expect in Ireland, not even a hint of it had been passed down to us in modern times. Indeed, it is very likely that there had been several layers of such lore – each subsequent layer superseding or modifying the beliefs of earlier inhabitants as new people came to live in the area in later Bronze Age and Iron Age times, bringing with them their own particular religious stories and cults. I came to the inescapable conclusion that what stories had to have existed in the past must have been deliberately suppressed; indeed censored!

But who might have done such a thing? One clue can be found in the name of the mountain itself – modern Irish *Aireagal*, anglicised as Errigal.

In today's more secular Ireland each individual has a first name and a surname. But in the more credulous times of the 1950s and 1960s when I was a child, "first names" did not exist – at least in our cultural contexts. No! we had "Christian" names to go with our surnames. Aireagal is just that, literally a "Christian" name. According to the Royal Irish Academy's authoritative *Dictionary of the Irish Language based mainly on Old and Middle Irish materials*, the word Aireagal (Old Irish *Airecal*) is derived from the gaelicisation of the

Latin word *oraculum*, meaning originally "a place where an oracle [a response from a divinity] is given". In early medieval Ireland that word seems to have acquired the secondary Christian meaning of "oratory". In origin – in the classical world from where it came – the word *oraculum* would have had purely pagan connotations. But Latin was introduced to Ireland through the medium of Christianity, newly arrived here during the fifth century AD from within the declining Roman Empire where it was by then the official state religion. We can be fairly confident that as a variant of the Latin word *oraculum*, Airecal / Aireagal / Earagail / Errigal is a name which postdates the introduction of Christianity to this island. Indeed, the name itself is almost certainly a Christian "artefact", although it clearly hints at the hallowed role the mountain must have had had before the arrival of the new religion. It would appear therefore – although, of course, we have no way of proving it because no relevant contemporary documentation survives – that the mountain was literally "christened" Airecal, just as the people who lived at its base were being christened in baptism as they made the transition from their old pagan beliefs to the newly introduced Christian religion.

Such a scenario would explain the name of the mountain but not the absence of traditional lore about it – indeed, the total silence concerning whatever beliefs existed regarding it before the arrival of Christianity. Why is this? Elsewhere in Ireland, perhaps most famously in the example of Croagh Patrick mentioned above, the older traditions about that mountain and even the cult practices performed on it were given a Christian veneer and absorbed into the culture of the new religion. The complete absence of such things for Errigal could only have been achieved through deliberately intended censorship. And only the priesthood of the new religion, once they were established, would have had the authority and influence – the "power" – to achieve that. But why would they have done such a thing?

It is now well accepted that the traditional Christian stories and practices associated with, for example, Croagh Patrick are a transmogrification of much older beliefs associated with the powerful pagan god Lug, or Lugh Lamhfhada as he is better known in Ireland.[2] Lugh is not connected – at least overtly – to the name of Errigal or, obviously, to the non-existent traditions about the mountain. But his name is preserved in the placename Dún Lúiche/Dunlewey at the foot of the mountain on its southern side, and in the name of the lake – Loch Dhún Lúiche – immediately adjacent. Indeed, Lugh, through the stories told about him and his evil adversary Balor, is an almost constant – even a ghostly – presence in the area of northwest Donegal dominated by Errigal.[3] That area comprises the districts of Gaoth Dobhair and Cloch Cheann Fhaola and the islands off the coast extending out to Tory. In the sixth, seventh, and eighth centuries that area formed the territory of the little kingdom of Síl Lugdach (see below). I will return below also to what might have been the original *dún* of Dún Lúiche. But I should make it clear at this stage that I believe that the awesome presence of Errigal used to be understood in some way as a mysterious manifestation of the god Lugh himself or, at very least, as a physical "path" for those who wished to "approach" him.

Beliefs about and devotion to Lugh, of course, were not confined to northwest Donegal or even to Ireland. Known by some variant of the name Lugus or Lugos, he was a favourite European god in Iron Age times, whose name is still preserved in placenames right across the western parts of the continent. The modern city of Lyon in central France, for instance, takes its name from a contraction of the ancient form Lugudunon/Lugudunum, meaning exactly the same thing as Donegal's Dún Lúiche – "the fort of [the god] Lug".[4] Laon in France, Leiden in Holland, Lugo in the Galician territory of Spain, possibly Leuven or Louvain in Belgium, the ancient Caer Luguvalos (what is now Carlisle) in England), Ludgate Hill in London where St Paul's Cathedral stands – as well as many other places – probably served in those times as sanctuaries of some sort dedicated to the god Lug. In Ireland the ancient tribal name Luigni – derived from some kind of "totemic" association with the god, survived apparently in placenames such as (possibly) Dunloy in County Antrim, Leyny in County Sligo and Lune in County Meath.[5] Lug was commemorated also in Lú, the name in Irish of what is now County Louth,[6] as well as in several other places. In Ireland, stories (sometimes the same or similar stories) about him were rooted in diverse places in a manner parallel – at least in some respects – to the beliefs about the Virgin Mary that are found in separate apparition places and shrines around the world. Similarly with Lugh, we don't have to expect any exclusiveness – or even consistency – in the stories about him. In ancient times long-distance communications were almost non-existent by our standards and different stories arose in different places about the same character, or the same story became separately localised, as it were, in different places.

In ancient times northwest Donegal was very remote – definitely from places such as central France where Lug's cult was strong, but even from other parts of Ireland separated by the wall of mountains to its east and south. Errigal is the highest peak of those mountains. So how did Lug's cult get there? In those times when roads were primitive or non-existent transport by water was tremendously important. The ocean was the common highway of the time. Because of the details reproduced in what is called Ptolemy's "map" of about 150 AD, we know that by then some knowledge of the Atlantic coast of Donegal existed within the Roman Empire, even as far east as Egypt from where Ptolemy came from. There is even a scatter of what are often called sub-Roman objects – that is "cheap" Roman or Roman imitation objects – found along the coast of Cloghaneely, from Ballyness to Dunfanaghy. One explanation for the occurrence of these objects is that they were traded with the "natives" for the peculiar white sand to be found on the northern slopes of Muckish; sand which is excellent for glassmaking.[7] The Romans were great glassmakers, but it was always understood that this occurred only in the eastern Mediterranean area. However recently rare evidence for what appears to be Roman glassmaking has been found in York in the north of England. The Muckish quarries might have provided the raw material for the latter industry. Indeed, one explanation for the name Dunfanaghy and the similarly named people who lived in its vicinity as marked on Ptolemy's "map" is that these were known as something like the "white people" or "people of the white territory", a name possibly derived from the fact that they were the custodians of the adjacent glowing white sand. If any of this was true, then such a trade-route may have been how a western European cult centred on Lug got transferred to northwest Donegal. As we will see below, Lug was deemed to be the equivalent of the Roman god Mercury who, pertinently in this context, presided over trade and commerce and whose name gave us the word "merchant".

So who or what was this Lug or Lugh?

In our time we are probably best acquainted with his cult because of the name Lúnasa in Irish for what in English and most other European languages is the month of August. The latter was named about 8 BC for Augustus, the first Roman Emperor – Gaius Julius Caesar Octavianus – but the Irish language preserves an older form. Lúnasa (Old Irish: Lughnasadh) was the name of what used to be one of the greatest annual festivals held in all (or most) parts of Ireland, just as (known by cognate names) it was almost certainly similarly an important festival in other parts of western Europe before the arrival of the Romans and later of Christianity.[8] Lughnasadh was one of the four so-called "quarter days" of the solar year.[9] It fell halfway between the summer solstice and the autumn equinox and marked the end of the summer growing season and the beginning of the harvest. In modern times Lug has sometimes been interpreted as a sun god although that now seems unlikely.[10] However, his connection with, as it were, the "fruits" of the sun – that is, the harvest – seems unassailable.

The eight ancient festivals of the solar year, following each other at regular intervals, were as follows:

1. Samain at the beginning of November, later Christianised as Halloween and All Saints Day, marked the beginning of winter and the new "Celtic" year. It fell halfway between the autumn equinox and the winter solstice.

2. The winter solstice, conventionally marked on 21 December but shifted a few days by the Christian church to Christmas (formerly the Roman festival of *Sol Invictis*).[11]

3. Imbolc at the beginning of February, later Christianised as St Brigid's feastday, marked the beginning of spring and fell halfway between the winter solstice and the spring equinox.

4. The spring equinox, conventionally marked on 21 March. One variation in medieval times saw the year change on 25 March (rather than 1 January), a slight shift of the official equinox date similar to the shift at Christmas;

5. Bealtaine or May Day, marking the beginning of summer, fell halfway between the spring equinox and the summer solstice. It was dedicated by the Christian church to the Virgin Mary.

6. The summer solstice, conventionally marked on the 21 June but shifted especially in Ireland, to 23/24 June as St John's Eve and feastday.

7. Lughnasadh at the beginning of August and falling halfway between the summer solstice and the autumn equinox marked the end of the summer growing season and the beginning of the harvest. Because of its popularity and that of the god after whom it was named, the festival persisted in Ireland long after the introduction of Christianity. It did not get a particular religious makeover but was marked, for instance, by pseudo-Christian practices and rituals (see below).[12]

8. The autumn equinox, conventionally marked on 21 September but in reality falling a few days later. Whether purely a coincidence or not, 23 September is the feastday of the very important and genuinely historic Donegal saint: Adomnán, Adhamhnán or Eunan.

In her great book, *The Festival of Lughnasa*, Máire Mac-Neill showed how traces of that ancient festival had survived in various ways right down to the middle of the twentieth century, including in the area around Errigal. Those survivals were not just archaeological, in the sense that ancient remnants remained the origins of which could be reconstructed, but that living aspects of the festival itself persisted into modern culture. There were (and indeed still are) various manifestations of, and names for that festival in different parts of Ireland, of which perhaps the most spectacular still is the annual pilgrimage on the last Sunday of July to the "Reek" or Croagh Patrick in County Mayo. There, the original pagan solemnities – doubtless organised in late prehistoric times in honour of the god Lug – were Christianised in the Middle Ages in honour of St Patrick.

Proinsias Mac Cana claimed that the name of the god Lugus meant something like "The shining one" (in Irish, "an té a lonraíonn").[13] Several scholars suggested that it was cognate with the Latin word *lux*, "light", although others rejecting that connection linked it instead with an ancient Celtic word *lugio* meaning an oath.[14] Whatever its actual etymology Mac Cana concluded that:

> Not only is it virtually certain that [Lugus] was known to all the Celtic peoples, but he is analogous in several respects, notably in his use of magic, to the Germanic Odin and the Indian Varuna. His usual epithet [in Irish], Lámhfhada, "of the long arm" may refer to his mode of fighting (with throwing spear and

sling), but it has also been compared with the similar epithet of the Indian god Savitar, "of the wide hand", who stretches out his hand to control sun, moon and stars and to regulate the succession of day and night. In short there is no good reason to suppose that Lugh does not belong to the Indo-European heritage.[15]

Even some academics who professed scepticism about these alleged international connections and comparisons are happy to acknowledge that "Lug is undoubtedly ... a pagan Celtic deity in origin".[16]

Professor Mac Cana had argued:

> That [Lug] was in fact the most honoured of the [Celtic] gods seems to be confirmed by the archaeological evidence. His inscriptions and monuments are more numerous than those of any other god, so that [Julius] Caesar evidently spoke truly when he reported that "huius sunt plurima simulacra" ("the images of this god are very many").[17]

Caesar had written that the ancient Gauls reckoned that their deity whom he recognised as the equivalent of the Roman god Mercury (who was, in turn, the equivalent of the Greek god Hermes) was "the inventor of all arts and a guide on the roads and on journeys ... and the most influential for money-making and commerce." Although Caesar did not record the name by which that god was known, many scholars believe that he can be equated with Lug. Caesar's phrase – "omnium inventorem atrium", "the inventor of all arts" – echoes one of Lug's principal epithets in Old Irish texts: Samildanach, "skilled in many arts", at least some of which he was claimed to have "invented" himself.

Like the classical gods Mercury and Hermes, in Proinsias Mac Cana's words Lug was "youthful, athletic and handsome". Many Irish references describe his bodily beauty, representing him as a king of the otherworld and as the "divine prototype of human kingship". In verses written by the fourteenth-century poet Gofraidh Fionn Ó Dálaigh, Lug is described in the following manner:

> To match in beauty him who stands there
> were a cause for slowness,
> no creature made of earth or water
> yet can dare it.
> His face, his hair, his body,
> key of choosing,
> like blood and bronze, and lime for whiteness
> is the triad.

His tongue is sweeter

than lute-strings finely fashioned

for gentle sleep

and ever played by expert fingers.[18]

Another description of the god Lug – in the early visionary text *Baile in Scáil* – says: "There was never in Tara a man of his size or his beauty, on account of the fairness of his form and the wondrousness of his appearance".[19] His reputation as Lámhfhada ("long-armed") reflected his skill with javelins and spears and echoes his equivalence with Lleu Llawgyffes ("accurate arm") in Welsh tradition.

One of the principal stories about the god empha-sises his killing of his maternal grandfather, the tyrant Balor. Dáithí Ó hÓgáin compared this with similar stories from Mediterranean, Persian and Babylonian mythology.[20] The tyrant in these latter mythologies was often identified as some variant of Taranos, the thunder-god. But in Irish tradition (and notably in the traditions of west Donegal) he was represented as Balor of the Evil Eye.[21]

Lug makes a relatively large number of appearances in ancient Irish texts and modern folklore although, perhaps unfortunately (but understandably), collec-tively these do not present a totally reconciled or coherent narrative. It is evident that many different stories about the god were in circulation in Ireland in late prehistoric and early historic times. The most detailed and "classical" account of Lug as an Irish character can be found in the text *Cath Maige Tuired* or "The [second] Battle of Mag Tuired".[22] That text was described by James Carney as "the most important Irish mythological tale",[23] but Kim McCone has shown how it exhibits various biblical parallels and probable influences, most notably in the similarities between Lug and King David.[24]

> ... Lug's good looks, many talents, skills on the harp, valour, judgement and ability to slay a Fomorian giant [Balor] with a slingshot bear an uncanny likeness to the attributes of that slayer of the Philistine Goliath and paragon of Old Testament kingship David that is hardly all due to coincidence.[25]

The account of Lugh in the *Cath Maige Tuired* is the most elaborate surviving ancient version of his story – the classical version. But northwest Donegal has its own localised version. Although different in detail, the Donegal account parallels several aspects of the story in *Cath Maige Tuired*, most especially the explanation of how the good god Lugh comes to kill the evil god Balor, his grandfather. The Donegal version was first recorded in writing by John O'Donovan of the Place-names' Section of the Ordnance Survey in a letter he wrote from Ballyconnell House in Falcarragh on 17 September 1835.[26] Although written by O'Donovan in English, he had heard the story narrated by Seán Ó Dúgáin, a native of Tory Island who almost certainly recounted it in Irish.

That version tells how Balor who lived on Tory had one daughter, Eithne. As he had been warned by a druid that he would be killed by his grandson, Balor locked Eithne away to ensure that she could never get pregnant. But, in the manner of such stories, Eithne did encounter a male consort, whom O'Donovan called MacAneely – the anglicised folk eponym of the place-name Cloghaneely.[27] MacAneely fathered triplet boys on Eithne. Only one, Lugh, survived and he was reared on the adjoining Donegal mainland. In time, out of revenge, Balor came across the sound from Tory and killed MacAneely on a stone (*cloch*) still to be seen in Falcarragh to the present day! Ultimately in revenge for this Lugh killed Balor in turn – in different places according to separate versions of the story. In one version he is killed at Drumnatinny on the coast near Falcarragh where MacAneely is said to have been connected with a forge. In other variations, on his death the ulcerous contents of Balor's evil eye carved out the eponymous Poison Glen (Cró Nimhe) in Dún Lúiche at the foot of Errigal, or alternatively split the huge glacial boulder known as Cloch Hatán at the entrance to the Glen.

Ó Dúgáin's nineteenth-century story seems to be a slightly distorted folk version of an ancient origin tale designed to explain the existence of the little kingdom in the area known in early medieval times – sixth to eighth centuries – by the dynastic name Síl Lugdach ("the seed of" or "descendants of Lugh") and probably in earlier times by the tribal name Luigni, meaning more or less the same thing. That kingdom remained small and isolated (and maybe even still pagan) up to about 725 AD when it began to expand to the north and east. By the ninth century it had expanded into the much better agricultural lands of east Donegal. In the later Middle Ages, under its leading families the O'Dohertys and the O'Donnells, leaving their original homeland behind them, they would take over the whole of what is now County Donegal. But the original Síl Lugdach territory, even to the present day, remained steeped in the lore of the god Lugh. The awe-inspiring peaked mountain on the southern borders of that orig-inal kingdom – Errigal – was almost certainly a major physical aspect of the cult of the god, perhaps in some mystic way imagined as an actual manifestation of him. The mountain probably had a name which reflected that – such as Sliabh Logha – before it was "christened" with the new Christian name Airecal. As part of that "conversion" process and because the cult of the god was so strong and pervasive in the area, it was necessary for the clergy of the new religion to suppress, as much as possible, all the traditions, stories and rituals connected with Lugh, leaving the mountain bereft of its ancient lore and, effectively, without a recorded past – oral or written. Whether it was linked to that cultural cataclysm or not, the cult of Lugh did continue to manifest itself down to the mid-twentieth century in a much tamer and more limited way on Carn Tra-onach mountain to the west of Errigal, just across the Gleann Átha valley, and on Beltany Hill to the north.

Errigal is located on what would have been the southeast border of the Síl Lugach territory. It was that kingdom's "south pole" in a way that Tory, nine miles off the coast, was its "north pole"! In the stories, in so far as we can reconstruct them, Errigal seems to have been characterised as the counterpart and even, in some ways, the nemesis, of Tory. Errigal was land, Tory was sea; Errigal was sunrise, Tory sunset; Errigal was high, Tory low; Errigal often looked white(ish), Tory often looked black(ish); Errigal was good(ish), Tory bad(ish), etc. Those two extraordinarily dramatic-looking geographical entities – the mountain and the island – symbolised in some ways all the cosmic opposites that could be imagined. Those qualities were fictionalised in the characters of their presiding deities – the old, evil, ugly Balor from Tory, and the young, good, beautiful Lug (almost certainly) from Errigal. Dún Baloir on Tory as opposed to Dún Lúiche at Errigal.

Dún Baloir is a well-known and clearly visible ancient monument (a promontory fort, formed of earthworks and other features) at the east – the "towery" – end of Tory.[28] Standing inside the fort and looking south you are directly confronted across the sound by Errigal rising proud on the mainland. You could be forgiven for imagining them as two mythological "boxers", each sizing the other up before any punch is thrown. But where or what exactly was the more elusive Dún Lúiche – Lug's fort? Several possibilities and suggestions exist, such as the site of the house now known locally as Teach a' Dúin on the south side of Loch Dhún Lúiche – although Tory is not visible from that location; or the stronghold known as An Dúnán[29] at the northwest foot of the mountain from which the enemy – Tory – is fully visible. But perhaps a conundrum outlined at the outset of this essay might provide another answer. As we have seen above, the name Errigal derives from the early Christian era when – at least officially – the cult of the god Lugh was suppressed including, apparently, the pre-Christian name of the mountain. Could the mountain itself have been the original Dún Lúiche, the local 'home' of the god Lugh? B'fhéidir!

Ach b'fhéidir fosta nach mbeidh muid cinnte go deo!

Dunlewey, Co Donegal

Endnotes

1 R.L. Praeger, *The Way That I Went*. Dublin 1937; reprinted Dublin 1980, p. 30.

2 See especially M. MacNeill, *The Festival of Lughnasa*. Oxford 1962; reprinted Dublin 2008, pp. 71-84.

3 For an accessible modern retelling of the story in both English and Irish see C. Ó Searcaigh, S. Ó Gaoithín & S. Fitzgerald, *Lugh na bua – Lugh the Deliverer*. Oxford 2017.

4 D. Mac Giolla Easpaig, "Places and early settlement in County Donegal" in W. Nolan, L. Ronayne & M. Dunlevy (eds), *Donegal, History and Society*. Dublin 1995, pp. 149-82, pp 154-5.

5 E. Hogan, *Onomasticon Goidelicum*. Dublin 1910; reprinted Dublin 1993, pp. 507-8; Mac Giolla Easpaig, "Places and Settlement", p. 155.

6 A. Ó Maolfabhail, *Ó Lyon go Dún Lúiche*. Dublin 2005, p. 76.

7 J. Cahill Wilson, B. Lacey & S. McGlade, "A possible context for Roman finds from west Donegal", *Ulster Journal of Archaeology*, 74 (2017–18), 26-32.

8 M. MacNeill, *The Festival of Lughnasa*.

9 In the original territory of the Síl Lugdach there are a number of particular places associated apparently with each of these festivals. As listed below these were: Samain – associated with the later ecclesiastical site at Tullaghobegley, the feastday of whose presiding (but probably "invented") saint, Begley = Beg Laoch or even Beg Lugh, was 1 November; Imbolc can be associated more tentatively with Drumnatinney ("ridge of the fire") where there is said to have been a mythical forge. Imbolc was Christianised as the feastday of St Brigid who in her guise as a pagan goddess was the patron of smithwork and was associated with a fire cult; Beltaine (May Day) is the name of a prominent hill north of Errigal which is said also to have been the location for Lughnasadh celebrations into the twentieth century; Lughnasadh celebrations also took place into the twentieth century on the summit of Carn Traonach mountain northwest of Errigal. But it is the main argument of this essay that Errigal itself was probably the original principal locus of the cult of Lugh in the area in pre-Christian times.

10 For a full discussion of the suggestion that the stories about Lugh "can be interpreted quite sensibly as a veiled description of a comet", see P. McCafferty & M. Baillie, *The Celtic Gods: Comets in Irish Mythology*. Stroud 2005, especially pp. 44-50.

11 Quite apart from the need of the Christian church to emphasise its separateness from those originally pagan festivals, various adjustments to the calendar down the centuries have complicated the situation slightly and moved what would have been their actual dates by a few days.

12 However, it does seem likely that some of the widespread folk practices associated with 15 August – the Feast of the Assumption of Our Lady into Heaven or (in Irish) Lá Fhéile Muire san Fhómhar – owe their origins, at least partly, to those performed for the ancient festival of Lughnasadh.

13 P. Mac Cana, *Celtic Mythology*. London 1970, p. 74.

14 D. Ó hÓgáin, *The Lore of Ireland*. New York & Cork 2006, p. 311.

15 *Celtic Mythology*, p. 29.

16 For example, K. McCone, *Pagan Past*. Maynooth 1991, ix and p. 158.

17 *Celtic Mythology*, p. 27. In contradiction of this, however, it has to be said that images of Lug/Lugh are generally absent in Ireland. One piece of ancient sculpture, now at St Patrick's Church of Ireland cathedral in Armagh, is sometimes claimed as a depiction of him.

18 "Tadhbhás Do Lugh, Leannán Teamhra", edited and translated by J. Carney, *Medieval Irish Lyrics*. Dublin 1967, pp. 88-91.

19 Translated by R. Thurneysen as quoted in E. Bhreathnach, *The Landscape and Kingship of Tara*. Dublin 2005, p. 40.

20 *The Lore of Ireland*, p. 312.

21 For Balor's connection with thunder and lightning see Ó hÓgáin, *The Lore of Ireland*, pp. 28-9.

22 E. Gray (ed.), *Cath Muige Tuired*. London 1982.

23 J. Carney, "Language and Literature to 116", in D. Ó Cróinín (ed.), *A New History of Ireland I: Prehistoric and Early Ireland*. Oxford 2005, pp. 451-510, p. 464.

24 See K. McCone, "A tale of two ditties: poet and satirist in Cath Maige Tuired", in D. Ó Corráin, L. Breathnach & K. McCone (eds), *Sages, Saints and Storytellers: Celtic Studies in Honour of Professor James Carney*. Maynooth 1989, 122-43, p. 138.

25 *Pagan Past*, p. 159.

26 See M. Herity (ed.), *Ordnance Survey letters, Donegal*. Dublin 2000, pp. 39-44.

27 The placename almost certainly actually derives from a real historical person, rather than a fictional mythical or folklorish character – a king of the Síl Lugdach called Cenn Fáelad who died around the first few decades of the eight century. See B. Lacey, *Lug's Forgotten Donegal Kingdom: The Archaeology, History and Folklore of the Síl Lugdach of Cloghaneely*. Dublin 2012, pp. 39-41.

28 B. Lacy (ed.) *Archaeological Survey of County Donegal*. Lifford 1983, pp. 226-7.

29 This is a prominent raised outcrop of rock, described as an "earthwork" (42.3) in the list of recorded monuments, and as "ringfort – unclassified" on archaeology.ie. While the site certainly would have been suitable as an ancient enclosure/fortification, there is not much on the surface there now that can be interpreted as archaeological features.

RÚN BUÍOCHAIS

Ba mhaith liom buíochas ó chroí a ghabháil leo seo a leanas as tacaíocht leanúnach thar na blianta : Ealaín na Gaeltachta; Séamas Ó Gallchóir in Údarás na Gaeltachta; Traolach Ó Fionnáin, oifigeach ealaíne Dhún na nGall; Caitlín Ní Bhroinn, Pleanáil Teanga Chloich Cheann Fhaola agus le hÉamonn Ó Domhnaill as obair eagarthóireachta. Is mór an spreagadh a thugann siad ar fad domh agus mé i mbun saothar pinn. Is mian liom buíochas ó chroí a ghabháil le hÁine Ní Mhaoláine as clóscríbh a dhéanamh ar an leabhar seo.

Mo bhuíchas le Chris Agee, Jacob Agee agus an foireann ar fad ag Cló an Mhíl Bhuí.